Where Wine flows like Water

Where Wine flows like Water

A Gastronomic Pilgrimage
Through Spain

John McAneney

HarperCollins*Publishers New Zealand*

First published 1997
HarperCollins*Publishers (New Zealand) Limited*
P.O. Box 1, Auckland

ISBN 1 86950 237 X

Cover photography by Stephen Robinson
Cover design by Ben Archer
Illustrations by Helen Casey
Design and production by 2D Design Limited
Typesetting and artwork by HieroGraphics
Printed by GP Print Ltd, Wellington, New Zealand

$\mathcal{L}$ista des Menciones

$\mathcal{L}$eaving the family for six weeks of pilgrimage and wine-tasting one's way to salvation is a perilous business: the first week was great, the second a little harder; but by the end of a month and on the other side of the world, impartial witnesses claimed that our families had learnt to cope admirably with the absence of any father-figure. According to Delphine, everything ran more smoothly without my chaotic and irrational inputs. Tissie also alleges that Pete and I were both rather strange for the first 12 months following our return, but fortunately this wild assertion has never been put to the test in a court of law.

The realisation of this book was only possible with the help and support of a wide number of friends and inevitable sacrifices by my immediate family. Amongst our many friends in France, special thanks must go to Jean-Pierre Lagouarde, who together with those Españologues from Lagor, was largely responsible for demonstrating to us the difference between cooking for survival and pleasure. Many of the recipes in this book were first experienced in one form or another in the kitchens of Pierrette and Jeannette in Lagor, or *chez* Jean-Pierre in Bordeaux. Jean-Pierre was also an unerring source of advice, photographs and other sundry material on El Camino. In a similar vein, I am indebted to Blanca Lobrera Martinez and José-Luis Arrue Ugarte and their extended family for their long friendship, hospitality, and help in getting started on the Spanish leg of the pilgrimage.

My other main adviser on *haute cuisine* has been Delphine, who, except for having a bizarre aversion to possum, is prepared to give almost anything else a go. I am also indebted to Thierry and Hélène Boulard in Provence, and Françoise Wilson, Patricia Rivat, Dave Murray and Robyn Martin in New Zealand for recipes and advice.

I would also like to thank Sue Page and Ian Watt of HarperCollins (New Zealand) Limited, and my agent Gaby Naher (Hickson Associates, Sydney) for their respective contributions. I am also indebted to Helen Casey for her marvellous illustrations and cover design. My only complaint is that she has made Pete seem much more saintly than he deserves.

Lastly I must acknowledge Pete himself, without whose enthusiasm and unflagging cheerfulness the pilgrimage would have been a very different experience; and without the example of his determination to keep a diary, I would never have had the discipline to do the same.

Buvez bien, et que le bon Dieu vous tienne en joie!
John McAneney
Tapuaetahi 1996

Where am I?

Who am I?

How did I come to be here?

What is this thing called the world?

How did I come into the world?

Why was I not consulted?

And if I am compelled to take part in it,

Where is the director?

I want to see him.

Søren Kierkegaard

Contents

$\mathcal{L}$ist of Recipes

 *peritivo*

But let no one in this company, I beg,

If I should speak what comes into my head

Take anything I say amiss,

All that I'm trying to do is amuse.

(Canterbury Tales, *William Chaucer*)

'*Y*ou're crazy!'

'Why would anyone choose to walk a thousand kilometres? Have you never heard of the internal combustion engine?'

Such had been typical responses to my decision to follow an ancient pilgrimage trail on foot across the Pyrénées and northern Spain to Santiago de Compostela, the supposed site of the tomb of the Apostle Saint James.

Mid-life crisis? No way! While it was true that I was of that delicate age when many begin to take an inordinate interest in their own appearance and other men's wives, I'd countered that temptation by studiously avoiding growing up. This has been a deliberate choice based on the as yet unproven hypothesis that aging can be staved off indefinitely by increasing irresponsibility. Carl Jung opined, more or less, that a man was destined to spend his first forty years trying to find himself; thereafter he was condemned to live with this self-knowledge as well as his impending mortality. *C'est pas gai ça.* Delphine, my wife, an even more acute observer than Jung, alleges unfairly that I'd been going through a succession of mid-life crises for over ten years. I liked to put such wild accusations down to her monthly hormonal imbalances, but there was always the possibility that she was right. Well, such talk is leading us onto dangerous ground, so let's just concentrate on having a good time, unshackled by self-doubts and other sanctimonious twaddle. But first, a bit of history.

Some 12 or so years had elapsed between the death of Jesus and James's martyrdom in Jerusalem about AD 44 when he was put to the sword and beheaded by Herod Agrippa.[1] According to early reports, James had been evangelising in Spain and returned to Jerusalem at a time of persecution for the fledgling Christian church. It is said that a small group of followers recovered his remains and transported them to the coast where they came across a small boat prepared for sail but without a crew. They placed the body in a coffin, and the boat, directed by an angel, made its way across the sea to the ancient kingdom of Asturias, or what is now the province of Galicia in northwestern Spain. The boat sailed up the river Ulla, stopping at a spot now occupied by the university city of Santiago de Compostela. There the tomb remained forgotten until at the beginning of the 9th century, its presence was made known to a solitary hermit by a supernatural light. It was soon recognised as the tomb of Saint James, and a temple constructed on the site. Wonderful things began to happen, miracles and apparitions multiplied. This was the source of a series of stories which encouraged knights in their battles against the Moors, and sustained the morale of the legions of early pilgrims in whose footsteps we planned to follow.

Today it is difficult to imagine the impact that the discovery of the Apostle's tomb had on Christendom and its continued attraction over subsequent centuries for the millions who have followed the varied routes to Santiago de Compostela. It wasn't just clergy who made the journey, but kings, queens and popes and, as we shall soon see, farmers and scientists. While spiritual motives have always played a strong role in encouraging people to take up the pilgrim staff, it should be remembered that life in the Middle Ages, and especially in the countryside during northern European winters, was often pretty grim. Thus, the opportunity for adventure in sunny climes was probably as sufficient an inducement for many pilgrims then, as it continues to be for those heading for La Costa del Sol from factory towns in northern England today.

There were also financial incentives for pilgrimage: it was a good way of escaping creditors and hence the expression in Gascony, 'Loaded with debts like the pilgrims en route to Santiago.'

Debts were often frozen for the duration of the pilgrimage, and people from some parts of Europe could avoid ever paying taxes if they went away for a minimum of three years. Attractive as were these possibilities, they were rejected out of hand by both my bank manager and the Inland Revenue Department — a salutary lesson on the relative importance of financial and spiritual obligations in a market-led economy.

Then there were indulgences or forgiveness credits to be gained for past and future crimes, and the journey could also be part of a sentence imposed for a crime or indiscretion. In some cases, pilgrims were paid to go by others, who, in a moment of weakness, had promised God that they would visit the Shrine of Saint James on the condition that He intervene in their lives. If it were not possible to make the journey in person, then the promise could be fulfilled by proxy. If I'd been hoping to finance my voyage by such means, I should have been very disappointed — people today are mostly not into promising God anything, let alone anything as rash as gratuitous exercise.

As a scientist I was fortunate to have a job that allowed me to indulge my curiosity with few restrictions. Although rarely appreciated by my director, time spent in 'idle' undirected thought is not wasted, especially if it is accompanied by exposure to new experiences and ideas. Inspiration is rarely the result of deliberate planning and is as likely to occur whilst doing the dishes as it is at one's desk. A friend of mine claims to be most productive when he has nothing to do. Charles Darwin went for long walks each afternoon; perhaps if I were to walk continuously for several weeks, I too could make some amazing discovery — just one would be rather nice. Today there seemed little likelihood of irritating the Church quite as much as Darwin has. And talking about church, a period of contemplation and Bible study might allow me to make some sense of those fragments of religious thoughts that episodically trespass my sub-conscience. While comfortable with the basic tenets of Christianity, my faith was based on an intuitive belief in a poorly defined God, and my knowledge of Scripture abysmal. Perhaps this voyage would allow me the opportunity to clarify a few things.

I had casually mentioned my interest in the Road to Santiago, or *El Camino*, as it is called in Spanish, to a friend over a meal. This interest had been aroused by various indications to pilgrimage trails around

Bordeaux where I had once spent a sabbatical year. Back home in New Zealand, this curiosity had become a mild obsession mounting roughly in inverse proportion to the probability of my ever finding the money or time to do the walk. When I first broached the idea with Pete, the possibility seemed rather remote and we had discussed it in a rather desultory fashion. Later, when changed circumstances made the voyage a reality, Pete's reaction caught me by surprise,

'Sounds like a great idea! I think I'll come too. You don't mind do you?'

'Ahh, ah.'

'Right then, I'll just check it out with the family and get back to you.'

Twenty-four hours later...

'No problems, I've promised Tissie and the kids that I'll lose a bit of weight, do some serious Bible study, and get my mid-life crisis over and done with in the desert. I'm booking my tickets tomorrow. You are still coming aren't you?'

And so we were two. Our detailed plan, the product of 20 minutes' serious thought, was to meet up in Bordeaux, where I had some work obligations. From there we would make our way by means as yet undetermined to the town of Oloron Sainte Marie at the base of the French Pyrénées. Here we would begin our assault proper, walking, God willing, very roughly between 900 and 1000 kilometres to Santiago de Compostela in northwestern Spain. Sounds simple, if you say it quickly, and therein lies our tale.

# ℋors D'Oeuvres

I have noticed again and again since I have been in the church that lay interest in ecclesiastical matters is often a prelude to insanity.

(Decline and Fall, *Evelyn Waugh*)

ℬeginning in Bordeaux
June 4

ℐ had earlier contacted my friend Jean-Pierre about the possibility of staying with him in Bordeaux for a few days and had received the following tongue-in-cheek response.

'What a shock! This is the first time that we have ever seen a pilgrim from the Middle Ages announce himself by electronic mail. It is with pleasure that I can offer you hospitality. In the room the most propitious for meditation and serenity, you can prepare yourself for the trials that await you along the route. I will put at your disposal a simple bed of wooden planks and we can break the fast frugally each day with a daily ration of a crust of bread and a jug of fresh water.'

Well, I had arrived safely and with the strong hope that Jean-Pierre, who has inherited a family interest in gastronomy, might be prevailed upon to exercise his culinary skills with something more interesting than bread and water. In the 12th century Aymery Picaud had claimed that the pilgrim approaching Bordeaux was entering a region 'where the wine was excellent, fish abundant, but the language crude'. I was quite capable of providing the latter, Jean-Pierre would have to take responsibility for the first two.

It is Jean-Pierre and his family who must take primary responsibility for awakening in me an atrophied interest in the pleasures of the table. Equally impassioned by gastronomy, rugby, sculpture, bullfighting and photography, he has the air and physio-gnomy of a somewhat Bohemian rugby player. One of my warmest recollections is of Jean-Pierre, bare-chested, un-shaven, and otherwise resplendent in Basque beret, rugby shorts, espa-drilles and John Lennon sunglasses, seriously explaining the details of an experiment in Castille-La Mancha to a high-level scientific German delegation all precisely decked out in formal dress despite the rigours of a Spanish summer.

Jean-Pierre and I had picked up Pete yesterday at the railway station in Bordeaux, where he had arrived from visiting relatives in Switzerland. Let me complete the formalities by introducing my travelling companion more fully. I'd known Pete for a number of years: we attended the same church and shared a common devotion to another more widely patronised New Zealand institution — rugby. As a general rule, I do not particularly enjoy the taste of beer, but when watching or discussing rugby, a beer or three is absolutely indispensable, and Pete's portly shape showed prima facie evidence of a close association with this noble art form. So weighing in at the kick-off at 0.1 megagrams, having seven children at the last count, and part owner-ship in several hundred hectares of assorted citrus, kiwifruit, melons and other diverse interests agricultural, Pete was a remarkable all-round individual. Physically robust, amiable, and extremely convivial; attributes that would serve us well in our forthcoming adventures.

This morning, I had shown Pete around Bordeaux. We had bought a guide book, and a map of the Pyrénées — we were now close enough to the pilgrim trail that some minimal planning would not be inappropriate. However, our attentions were easily distracted away from the maps and literature of the southwest which accounted for only a small proportion of the stock: the shelves were dominated by cookbooks. The range of possibilities was amazing. I carefully selected one tome out of some several hundred, drooling momentarily over the idea of carrying this treatise of classic recipes with us to Santiago, feasting each evening on *haute cuisine* cleverly prepared over our little primus stove. One last salivating look at the ingredients convinced me that it would be more appropriate as a gift for my teenage daughter, Sarah, who, when not suffering from mild and insincere flirtations with vegetarianism, was seriously interested in food.

We rested in a café and enjoyed the scenery. French women are fantastic: sexy, entertaining and unashamedly feminine; from behind, it is often impossible to tell whether they are sixteen or sixty. I watched Pete's reactions closely, remembering an American friend's first encounter in a sidewalk café in Paris.

'We had just sat down and ordered a beer when one of the most beautiful girls that I had ever seen crossed over the road. Pausing on the pavement in front of the café, she cast a languid glance at the myriad of bus timetables. Her appearance created immediate mayhem. At their first glimpse of her, two waiters catapulted into each other, sending drinks and glasses crashing. No-one heard a thing! An arthritic old man, who had probably not walked without the aid of a cane in forty years, ran unsupported to help with her bags, whereas I, after only five minutes in France and speaking not a word of French, felt an irresistible urge to give advice on the bus schedule. Then at the eye of this cyclone of confusion, this Parisian Venus turned slowly and undulated out of our lives, completely oblivious to the chaos she was leaving behind.'

Our brief stay in Bordeaux coincided with the wedding of the son of our friends. So after lunch, and in view of Pete's promise to lose some weight, we walked some 10 kilometres to a nearby village for the church service. Clothed in pilgrim garb and closely resembling bushmen from the Australian outback — shorts, singlet, leather boots, Crocodile Dundee hats, and plastic bags full of groceries — we tried to look inconspicuous in the back of the church. As the wedding party filed out, I was recognised immediately by François and Michèle who insisted that we come to the reception. Apologies for our native costumes were summarily dismissed: '*C'est génial ça! Très original!*'

It is difficult to recall exactly what took place that afternoon except to note that our fancy dress did not seem to constitute the slightest impediment to the enjoyment of champagne, caviar canapés and general merriment.

Le fête de Pèlerins at the home of Jean-Pierre later that night was another riotous affair to celebrate our many friends' imminent return to 'normality' after our departure *en pénitence*. It is impossible not to enjoy oneself amongst people so uninhibited about having a good time; the conversation flows easily between men and women as jokes become more and more embellished. Someone gave a detailed psychological profile of Tintin's dog; this led to an impassioned debate about Anglo-Saxon prudishness, the confusion between pornography and eroticism, and the correct temperature to serve a camembert. Jean-Pierre regaled us with stories of his years in North Africa, whilst Pete and I, knowing nothing about any of these subjects, especially Anglo-Saxon prudishness, contributed vigorously to the conversation by drinking anything put before us.

By 2 a.m. it was time for dessert and with great ceremony, Jean-Pierre produced his apple cake of which he is justly proud.

'A friend in Avignon loves this cake because of the different sounds produced as the teeth bite through the contrasting textures of the caramelised exterior, the apple itself and the sponge-like consistency of the bits in between.'

This claim provoked a chorus of helpful suggestions of toilet noises that could round out the repertoire of this *gateau acoustique*.

'You know, Jean-Pierre, that with a little more #*%*!@ this cake could be promoted as a breakfast cereal. You might make your fortune.'

Memories of this conversation would later stimulate Jean-Pierre to send me the recipe in allegorical form based on allusions to classical music. I give here only the concluding line which roughly translated goes something like:

'And go easy on the artificial vanilla flavouring or the concert is likely to be dominated by the wind section.'

$\mathscr{B}$avarois de Saumon Fumé

Smoked Salmon Mousse

This custard sauce is a blend of egg yolks and milk stirred over heat until it thickens into a light cream. With the addition of gelatine and whipped cream it becomes a Bavarian cream. Smoked marlin makes a wonderful alternative to salmon. Try it with champagne!

Ingredients:

500 g smoked salmon	4 egg yolks
freshly ground pepper	300 ml milk
10 g gelatine	300 ml fresh cream

1. *Coarsely blend 400 g of the smoked salmon.*
2. *Carpet the bottom of the mould with slices of the remaining salmon.*
3. *Add a large pinch of pepper to the egg yolks then beat with a wire whip just to the point when the drips form a slowly dissolving ribbon. Don't go beyond this point or the eggs will go granular when combined with the warm milk.*
4. *Bring the milk just to the boil in a heavy-bottomed saucepan. Leave to cool for 5 to 10 minutes.*
5. *Mix the eggs into the milk. Place back over low heat and stir continuously with a wooden spoon until the custard thickens enough to coat the spoon with a light creamy layer. It must not boil!*
6. *Add the gelatine, mixing rapidly with fork.*
7. *Whip the cream using moderate speed at first and then high-speed until it takes on an unctuous consistency — don't overdo it!*
8. *Mix the blended salmon with ¹/₂ cup of the custard to form a smooth paste.*
9. *Mix the rest of the warm custard with the salmon mixture and then fold in the whipped cream.*
10. *Pour into the mould and leave in the refrigerator for 12 hours.*
11. *Carefully remove from mould and serve on a bed of lettuce leaves.*

$\mathscr{L}$apin à l'Alsacienne
Rabbit Alsatian-style

The combination of meat and pastry is well known in English cuisine.
It is less common in France, but here is one of Jean-Pierre's favourites,
a dish from Alsace in which the meat is steamed in wine. Two important prerequisites for success: first make sure that the pastry sticks to
the sides of the baking dish to form an airtight seal — otherwise the
meat will dry out; and secondly, use a casserole dish in which the pieces
of meat fit snugly together to cover the base — otherwise you will have
too much liquid.

Ingredients:

1 rabbit	5 or 6 rashers bacon or
prepared French mustard	smoked ham
1 clove garlic	2 glasses of a good quality
salt and pepper	white wine
2 fresh bay leaves	sufficient flaky pastry to cover
a branch of thyme	your casserole dish

1. *Cut the rabbit into serving-size pieces. Rub mustard liberally over each piece.*
2. *Rub the inside of an earthenware casserole dish with garlic. Place the pieces of
   meat in a single layer in the bottom — they should be tightly squeezed together. Sprinkle with salt and pepper. Place a rasher of bacon over each portion.*
3. *Add the bay leaves, thyme, and sufficient wine to bring the level of the liquid
   just up to that of the meat.*
4. *Cover the top of the baking dish with flaky pastry. Allow sufficient pastry to
   hang down over the sides of the dish so that you can make a good airtight seal
   and also so that the pastry does not sag and touch the meat. Moistening the
   outside lip of the dish will help the pastry stick to the sides.*
5. *Bake at 200 °C for 2 hours. As the wine begins to steam, the pastry should
   bulge up away from the meat which will cook in the vapour.*
6. *Serve with boiled potatoes.*

Gateau Acoustique
Jean-Pierre's Apple Cake

Picasso had his blue period and I'm currently going through a caramel one. Just throw the following ingredients together and relax over what remains of the cooking wine. The cake will be covered in a delicious brown glaze when unmoulded.

Ingredients:

For the caramel:	100 g sugar
½ cup sugar	1½ tsp baking powder
1 Tblsp water	1 egg
	1 tsp vanilla essence
For the cake mix:	75 g butter, melted
4 crisp medium-sized	**(Depending on the size of the**
tart apples	**apples you may have to**
100 g flour	**double the mix.)**

1. *Caramelise a metal baking dish as follows: heat the sugar over moderate heat in the mould with the water, swirling frequently until the syrup caramelises. Tilt the mould to cover the bottom and sides with a thin film of caramel. When it has ceased to run, place to one side.*
2. *Peel, core and slice apples.*
3. *For the cake mix itself, add the dry ingredients to a bowl, then beat in the egg with a wooden spoon before folding in the vanilla essence and melted butter.*
4. *Fold the apples into the cake mix and pour into the mould.*
5. *Place in lower third of a pre-heated oven (160°C).*
6. *Cook for 1 hour and 15 minutes.*
7. *Allow to cool, then invert and take out of mould.*

*L*agor and Reverie en Route

June 5

*J*ean-Pierre drove us to his parents' home in the Béarn. Lagor, I love. This tiny hamlet dotted along a ridge looks out towards the south over farmland to vistas of the Pyrénées. Two years earlier and together with most of the village, we had crammed into the kitchen of the home of Jean-Pierre's aunt, Jeannette, to watch the semi-final of the World Cup rugby — the warmth radiating from the cinders at the base of the huge kitchen fireplace, a ham hanging smoking in the chimney, and two shotguns above an ancient charred mantelpiece. *Quelle ambience!* A splendid afternoon marred only by the performance of the Australians, who defying tradition, probability theory and fair play, rather convincingly outplayed New Zealand.

Driving south from Bordeaux through small, isolated hamlets of Les Landes I could not help but recall the wonderful feeling of community that pervades some of these villages. As a family, we had once lived in a beautifully picturesque village in Provence. Perched on the side of a hill and dominated by a Romanesque church, much of the architecture of Chateauneuf de Gadagne dated back to the 14th century — a period when the Popes were in Avignon. Every month or so there would be activities involving a high proportion of the 1000 or so inhabitants: be it the four-day fête in summer; dancing till 2 a.m. at the school to celebrate the beginning and end of each scholastic year; the annual dance for returned servicemen; or a special spring fête which included a mock trial to lay to rest all the malignant spirits of winter.

During long summer evenings children roamed free under the collective eye of the village, playing hide-and-seek amongst the tortuous alleyways that wound themselves within the confines of the old village walls and to the vineyards beyond. Wednesdays — free from school — were devoted to soccer on the plane tree-ringed square. Serving as the goal was an early 17th century chapel built in appreciation of God's protection over the village during the Plague. From time to time, the children would interrupt their games and race to the fountain to quench their thirst, or, on very hot days, to jump right in. On our arrival, this fountain had been very clearly labelled as *eau non potable*, a sign which the children removed after sampling the water with no obvious ill-effects. Ten years later, the water was still drinkable.

At the heart of village life in Gadagne was the municipal policeman — le garde. Official duties included ensuring that each morning and

afternoon the children safely crossed the main road which lay between the old part of the village and the new school; unofficial duties included un-blocking drains and fixing washing machines. Jeannot arrived one evening to pass on a complaint against my then four-year-old son. Already a hardened criminal, Sean had been accused of tipping a bucket of cold water over a group of elderly women, whom he had cleverly identified as witches because of their black costumes. He thought that they were satanic; they were convinced he was the devil.

Formalities dealt with and apologies duly accepted, Jeannot accepted a glass of wine.

'You are going to be cold here in winter,' said he, casting an eye around the sparsely furnished room. 'I have two rugs at home. I think you could do with one of them.'

The next day he returned with a rug and a television set.

'It belongs to a friend in the village — he is away for a few months and you may as well profit from his absence.'

Thus was the beginning of an enduring friendship; thereafter, we enjoyed together a glass of *pastis* most evenings as Jeannot made his way home.

Next door had lived a very old lady, Marie. Her short-term memory was not the best and each morning we would have an almost identical conversation:

'Hello, have you just moved in?'

'Yes, we are from New Zealand.'

'Ah, the north of France. Any children?'

'Two.'

'Well, let them come over and try the grapes,' she said, pointing to the vine that the children had already stripped.

One day Delphine found Marie trying to buy meat at the post office. She gently helped her back across the busy road and across the square to the *épicerie*.

'*Messieurs-dames.*'

'*Bonjour Marie,*' echoed a chorus of voices.

'What would you like today?'

'Four stamps.'

'No problems,' replied the grocer, carefully selecting several nice lamb cutlets, a substantial portion of *saucisson*, a few potatoes, several ripe tomatoes and a lettuce. 'Anything else?'

'Yes, I'd like some envelopes, please.'

'OK,' said the grocer, adding a small slice of cheese to the shopping bag. 'Have a nice day.'

No money had changed hands.

'What a nice man,' said Delphine once outside the shop.

'Yes, I think he is new to the village.'

Lagor similarly held a host of fond memories, many of them gastronomic, including an evening of *Poule au Pot de Béarn*. And so it came to pass that we were fêted that very evening to an extraordinary meal on the terrace of Jean-Pierre's family home. Almost every dish had been created from either home- or locally grown products. Venison pâté, home-cured ham, roast duck, ice-cream and strawberries — all washed down with champagne, 23-year-old Pomerol, and vintage Calvados. I could look forward with pleasure to a retirement modelled on that of Jean-Pierre's parents, Jean and Pierrette — hunting, fishing, and only if absolutely unavoidable, gardening; but generally enjoying the pleasures of the table and a fine cellar.

While all countries have their share of culinary specialities, the dishes of fêtes and special occasions, the richness of regional cuisines in France is truly astonishing. Only here have the pleasures of the table been raised to an art form so that *haute cuisine* forms a reference, a benchmark, against which food and wine all over the world are judged. Naturally not everyone cooks well, but the general expectation is that one should eat well. This is a country where it is not considered eccentric to drive 100 kilometres for a meal in a restaurant of note.

With some effort, a modicum of creative endeavour, and access to good quality meat, vegetables and fruits, and wine, it is possible to reproduce many of the specialty dishes. What is harder to recreate is the ambience of the table where enjoyment of debate plays as important a role as the cuisine; guests may be invited purely on account of their wit, and the quality of their conversation. Food is not necessarily complicated, and even very modest meals, artfully conceived and tastefully presented, can form the basis of a memorable lunch or evening. In this manner, a very simple repast of wine, cheese and bread can often provide sufficient sense of occasion.

At the other extreme are the legendary marathon meals of first communions and marriages. Such epic feasts are really dangerous. Forget cholesterol and clogged arteries; as described by the Bishop of Poitiers in the 6th century, it is the digestive tract that is most at risk from overindulgence.

'Soon I had a stomach swollen like that of a woman about to give birth — the capacity of this organ to dilate was simply amazing. [I presume he was still talking about his stomach.] Thunder rumbled within, with frequent backfires whilst roaring winds from both the north and the south simply blew my entrails apart.'[2]

Perhaps this is why gluttony was sometimes considered a deadly sin.

$\mathscr{P}$oule au Pot du Béarn

Farmyard Chicken from the Béarn

A too literal English translation takes away some of the magic of this traditional, mid-winter dish from the kitchens of Jeannette and Pierrette (Jean-Pierre's aunt and mother). An old farmyard fowl must be used rather than a young hen which would just fall to pieces with the long cooking; I have also used wild turkey to give quite a different but still rather special flavour. Note that the bouillon is multi-purpose: some is drawn off prior to the completion of cooking and used to cook the rice which is served as an accompaniment to the main course; the rest is strained to provide a clear soup for the entrée.

Ingredients:

1 small cabbage	1 small onion
1 old farmyard hen	¹/₂ clove garlic
rice for 6 people	1 Tblsp chopped parsley
chopped grilled bacon	salt and pepper

For the stuffing:	*For the bouillon:*
250 g bread	500 g lamb flap
250 ml milk	8 carrots
2 chicken livers	4 turnips
2 eggs	4 leeks
250 g ham	1 medium-sized onion
several spring onions	salt and pepper

1. *Wash the cabbage, drop whole into boiling water for 10 minutes, then drain and leave to cool.*

2. *To make the stuffing, crumble the bread into a pan and add the heated milk; finely chop all the other stuffing ingredients and mix with the damp bread. Salt the interior of the fowl, and then insert two large spoonfuls of the stuffing mixture. Sew up the opening and truss the bird.*

3. *Detach about half a dozen of the exterior leaves of the cabbage and set them aside. Carefully open out the remaining leaves of the cabbage without stripping them off. Starting at the centre, distribute the stuffing between the leaves and press lightly to flatten it. Wrap the stuffed cabbage within the external leaves which had been set aside and then tie the bundle all together using some string.*

4. *In a large soup pot with high sides, put enough cold water to cover the fowl — but don't add the bird at this stage. Throw in the bouillon ingredients plus the stuffed cabbage and the neck of the hen. Bring to the boil and skim off the scum which rises to the top. Season to taste. Allow to bubble for 60 minutes on a low heat.*

5. *Add the fowl to the pot and continue boiling on low heat for another hour and a half. Check seasoning.*

6. *After 70 minutes drain off sufficient liquid to cook the rice.*

7. *Strain the bouillon and serve as a soup with a garnish of chopped grilled bacon for the first course. Meanwhile keep the chicken and vegetables warm. Then serve the carved chicken on a hot plate surrounded by vegetables, the stuffed cabbage cut in slices, and the rice as a side dish.*

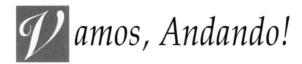

Vamos, Andando!

'Where are you going like that on your horse?'

'To Santiago de Compostela, my good lady.'

'Here, take some money, you can light a candle for me

at the altar of the Saint.'

(Priez Pour Nous à Compostelle,
P. Barret and J.N. Gurgand)

Oloron
June 6

*J*ean and Jeannette drove us to Oloron. Our 'official' starting point was to be the church of Sainte Marie with its magnificent 12th century

portal comprising a carved representation of Christ being taken down from the cross. Time has given the marble tympanum the appearance of yellowed piano keys. It is bounded by a semi-circle of carved figures all pursuing the day to day preoccupations of the Béarn — salmon fishing, preparation of cheese and hams, slaughtering ducks for the *foie-gras* and the *confit*, hunting and so on — all activities perpetrated under the disapproving eyes of the 24 austere old men of the Apocalypse. The entire portal is supported by a central sculptured column of two Saracen captives — chained back to back and condemned for eternity to support the Passion.

After some moments' reflection and prayer, we headed towards the Pyrénées following the river Aspe: trout fishing suddenly seemed a much more attractive recreational activity than walking to Compostela. The traffic was heavy, but there was little choice but to walk on the main road. Hot, humid and miserable, mist on the foothills obscured the true height of the mountains ahead. Just as well as our early euphoria was evaporating quickly.

Walking is often advocated as an ideal way of keeping fit provided that one begins slowly — a criterion we were having no difficulty satisfying. Village delicatessens provided welcome diversions and once inside, local specialities such as *confit de canard*, *daube de sanglier*, and *salmis de palombe* proved irresistible. The only problem was that each tin added an extra kilogram to Pete's already overladen pack. Mine, unfortunately, was already full — there are a lot of advantages to having a small pack. I promised myself to make amends later by eating more than my share.

At 5.30 p.m., we pitched the tent by the river after what had seemed like a very long first day. Dispirited and tired, we were uncertain of the actual distance that we had covered — maps, road signs, and our intuition all seemed at variance. Pete was already having trouble with his feet. To reach Jaca on Wednesday meant crossing the border tomorrow — and it was up, all the way!

A feast of bread and *confit de canard* restored our spirits. *Confit* is a speciality of the southwest of France: specially-fattened ducks used for the *foie gras* are cooked and preserved in their own fat. The same process can be used to make a very tasty dish from mutton. Afterwards I read the Bible while Pete carried out minor surgery on his feet. His blisters looked dreadful.

Although I had attended church for a couple of years on a semi-irregular basis since becoming a Christian — an act which some colleagues may imagine was due to my critical faculties being damaged by sitting too close to the organ — I had never really taken the time to read the Bible. With no other concerns except my feet, I decided to start at the beginning.

The Genesis description of the temptation and the fall of man is delightful in its description of the bickering that punctuates even the best relationships.[3] In this account of the entry of clothes, knowledge, and sin into the world, Adam blames both God and Eve, as he and his wife hide naked amongst the trees: 'That woman you put here with me, she gave me some fruit from the tree and I ate,' says he, affecting all innocence.

And so it was always the woman's fault! This seemed an indication that even marriages arranged by the Almighty were not without their difficulties. Pete and I had been discussing arranged marriages earlier in the day in relation to our daughters, some of whom were rapidly approaching that unmanageable age and becoming rather expensive to maintain at home. While they undoubtedly held fairly strong views on the subject, Pete and I had convinced ourselves that we would be able to make more appropriate choices. Perhaps we should reconsider.

As the light faded, we crawled into our sleeping bags. Sleep was slow in coming. It took hours to unwind leg muscles, which, like used rubber bands, had got all twisted up.

Confit de Mouton

Not quite the fattened goose but still amazing! — and faithful to the spirit of the French *confit*.

Ingredients:

2 kg lean mutton (a leg is ideal)
1 kg mutton flap (the sweet belly meat)
2 Tblsp salt
500 g lard

1. *Cut the lean meat into large cubes.*
2. *Cut up the flap but do not remove the fat.*
3. *Rub salt into the lean meat. Mix carefully and leave to sit for at least 2 hours.*
4. *Cook the pieces of flap for about 20 minutes in a large pot until the fat begins to melt.*
5. *Press the lean meat to express as much water as possible; pat dry with a cloth before adding to the pot.*
6. *Brown the meat well, adding the lard in small pieces.*
7. *Leave to cook for about 2 hours — the fat should be bubbling very gently and just covering the meat.*
8. *Leave to cool and then place in preserving jars. The fat must completely cover the meat — add an additional layer of melted lard if necessary. Cover the jar with a cotton top and store in a dry, cool environment.*
9. *Before serving, simply reheat and drain off the fat. Serve with potatoes fried in the same fat and try to forget about the calories.*

Pete would loose over the next four to five weeks of pilgrimage — it would have been far simpler, and more accurate, to adopt an empirical approach and weigh him before and after; but then prediction is the essence of science. Now it is said that the rate of energy expended during heavy work and fast walking is about 500 kcal/h in excess of food intake, i.e., 5000 kcal for a ten-hour day. Imagine for the moment that, with God's help, we could curb our natural inclinations, and maintain a dietary intake considered normal for an 80 (plus or minus 20) kilogram person, say around 3200 kcal per day. Then, if the difference were to be made up by the combustion of fat reserves, Pete (and I) should be burning off around 1800 kcal each day. This cruel calculation suggested a weight loss of roughly 200 grams a day, or approximately 1.5 kilograms every week. We would see later just how crude this estimate was.

I slept fitfully, dreaming that I had made an order of magnitude mistake in my calculations and Pete experienced melt-down before reaching Santiago. We were walking along and then he just sort of faded slowly away, like the smile on the face of the cat in *Alice's Adventures in Wonderland*. How would I explain his absence to his wife? Perhaps I could take back his shadow in a bottle and have it mounted in our church as a relic. There were precedents for this sort of thing — it wouldn't be quite the same as a vial containing the last breath of Christ, the tears of Mary Magdalene, or one of the many heads of John the Baptist, but then again the reliquary of our church was rather impoverished. I was just not sure this would be enough for Tissie. The whole issue would have to be handled with great sensitivity.

I wouldn't disclose these fears to Pete just yet. Given the state of his feet, he had enough to contend with.

*D*aube
Beef Casserole

Simple, flavourful and aromatic, the secrets of a successful daube are good ingredients, long, gentle, regular simmering so that the flavours and bouquet develop fully, and a heavy lid on the casserole dish — an old-fashioned camp oven is ideal to keep in the juices. Delphine has a preference for cooking red meat with a strongly flavoured white wine, but in the end it is a matter of personal taste. This recipe will also work with wild pig, but it is probably advisable to marinate the meat for 24 hours first and then cook it in the strained marinade with fresh vegetables. This dish will taste even better the next day after reheating.

Ingredients:

1¹/₂ kg shank or shoulder of beef (the working muscles and the cheapest cuts)	2 cloves
	¹/₄ cup olive oil, extra
	¹/₃ cup wine vinegar
3 cloves garlic	500 g carrots, cut in quarters
2 Tblsp flour	1 bouquet garni
2 Tblsp brandy	a good pinch of nutmeg
1 litre red wine	peel of 1 orange
2 Tblsp lard	8 grains of pepper
2 Tblsp olive oil	salt to taste (about 1 heaped tsp)
100 g bacon, cut in small cubes	3 or 4 ripe tomatoes
4 medium-sized onions	

1. *Cut the meat into large cubes and mix vigorously with the garlic. Sprinkle with flour.*
2. *Heat the brandy and wine together on the stove and flambé. Set to one side.*
3. *Brown the meat and garlic in the oil and lard in a heavy cast-iron casserole dish. When the meat just begins to catch, lower the heat and add the bacon, and onions studded with cloves. Fry slowly together*

adding a bit more oil if needed. Pour over the wine and brandy mixture,
extra olive oil and wine vinegar.

4. *Add carrots, herbs, nutmeg, orange peel, pepper and salt, and simmer for*
   3 hours in a tightly covered casserole dish.
5. *Add the quartered tomatoes and continue to simmer uncovered for*
   another hour or so until cooked, as indicated by the wonderful aromas
   that inevitably permeate the kitchen.
6. *Remove the bouquet garni, and serve the casserole on a heated plate*
   either surrounded with golden brown chips or accompanied with
   macaroni.

$\mathcal{J}$aca or Bust
June 8

$\mathcal{M}$ist lingering in the valleys provided a mystical backdrop to breakfast. Submerged in the physical beauty of our surroundings, we luxuriated on fresh melon and coffee. The morning collect was 'Jaca or bust'. There we would meet up with two close friends from university days: José-Luis, one of the most generous people I knew, and Blanca, petite and curvaceous, and with beautiful, dark Moorish looks.

We set off in high spirits, expecting an easy day, but it quickly turned into an endurance test at least as dispiriting as the first. The original pilgrim trail, which wound through scrub and low forest bordering the river, had to be abandoned after a short experiment as the uneven terrain aggravated Pete's blisters. Back on the tarseal, he cut bits and pieces off his boots at every stop in a valiant but unsuccessful attempt to make them more flexible. Soon he would be cutting bits off his feet to make them fit the boots.

The arrival of Canfranc provided a good excuse for rest and coffee. Its international railway station, a once magnificent building, was now in slow, smouldering decay since a runaway wagon destroyed a bridge and blocked rail communications between Spain and France some 30 years earlier. Ecologists wanted the route reopened, but it was claimed that the line was uneconomic. Recent notices and graffiti protesting against new plans to reconnect Spain and France with a motorway implied that the issue was not dead. With two days of walking under my belt, I'd already developed a healthy contempt for motorists, and as a consequence could not but sympathise with the protest view — why vandalise yet another beautiful valley just to speed up traffic flow for the benefit of business people in Zaragoza and Bordeaux? Locals stood to gain nothing except a few labouring jobs during the construction period. At risk was the destruction of a lifestyle and further degradation of one of the last refuges in the Pyrénées of the European brown bear. There were enough roads already!

We finally arrived outside José's holiday apartment in Jaca feeling like a couple of cripples; calf muscles stiff with pain, we lay down on the grass and dozed. José and Blanca arrived soon after to an emotional reunion. Pete looked a bit aghast; he was at this point still a bit unsure about overt displays of emotion between men — in New Zealand, they could easily be misinterpreted. Given a few more weeks in the company of Southern Europeans, I was confident that he would overcome this small inhibition with the same gusto that he had displayed in adapting to French wines.

By evening, we had both recovered to the point where it was possible to introduce Pete to a special Spanish experience — tapas. Consumed while standing at the bar and lubricated with frequent glasses of wine and congenial conversation, tapas vary from very simple fare to gastronomic gems. Originally from Andalucía, this finger food is now to be found throughout Spain and, in some towns, bars compete with one another for the best display. Thus, one can spend a rather expensive but thoroughly enjoyable evening with friends just walking between bars and sampling the varied choices. Here in Jaca, one of our favourite bars serves only baked potatoes with a special sauce — the only problems are firstly getting close enough to the bar to order, and secondly, inveigling the recipe from the patron.

During the skiing season, at 2 a.m. with the air temperature hovering at around –2 °C, streets and bars are often so swollen with people that it is almost impossible to walk anywhere directly. Rather, one just enjoys the animation of the crowd and succumbs to its collective spirit. Tonight, off-season, it was raining heavily and Jaca was empty.

$\mathscr{P}$atatas al Estilo de Jaca

Variation on a Theme from a Bar in Jaca

This is the closest we can get to the secret formula from one of our favourite bars in Jaca. The patron refuses to divulge the secret of his business success, the key to which lies with the vinaigrette sauce. This is Delphine's version .

Ingredients:

potatoes	mustard
garlic	salt
wine vinegar	pepper
vegetable oil	butter

1. *Bake potatoes in their jackets.*
2. *Meanwhile, make a simple sauce of very finely chopped garlic steeped in wine vinegar and vegetable oil in the ratio of 1 to 3, adding mustard, salt and pepper to taste.*
3. *Cut the potatoes in half, score the top with a fork, smear with butter, sprinkle with salt and grill until golden.*
4. *Drizzle the sauce over the grilled potatoes and serve hot.*

ⅅepression à la Zaragoza
June 9

𝒜 busy day beginning with church and communion. Jaca was once an important pilgrimage stop and to enter the 11th century cathedral is to be transported back some eight centuries to an epoch when the hopes of all Christendom centred on this tiny kingdom of Aragon and that of Asturias further to the west. From these two kingdoms began the struggle to wrest Spain back from the Moors. The heavy, dark architecture of the church conjured up images of Spanish knights receiving dispensation from attending battles in the Middle East in order to concentrate on their own crusade.

Next on the programme was a visit to San Juan de La Peña, a short car ride from Jaca. This tiny 8th century monastery is built into the side of the cliff and dominated by an immense overhang of rock. The Holy Grail — the chalice which Jesus used at the Last Supper — is said to have been kept here. From the cloister, with its columns carved with biblical scenes, are superb views of the Pyrénées, and in the foreground, eagles and vultures, wings outstretched, hitchhike effortlessly on rising thermal currents of air.

The origins of San Juan de La Peña predate the pilgrimage to Santiago: in 732, a youth from Zaragoza out hunting was galloping in pursuit of a stag when the deer fell over the cliff. The youth had been following so closely that both he and his horse would have suffered the same fate had not he the presence of mind to pray quickly to Saint John, whereupon his horse miraculously stopped at edge of the precipice. Dismounting, the young man scrambled down the rock face through the scrub, eventually coming across the stag lying dead at the entrance to a deep cave. Venturing inside, he discovered a tiny shrine, and lying in front of it, with his head resting on a stone, the body of an old hermit — Juan de Atarés. The young man buried the hermit and, following the dead man's example, sold all his possessions and went with his brother to live in the cave. After their deaths, the hermitage was continued by two disciples; later there would be up to 300 monks living and praying there.

Blanca's family is from this region, and lunch was a barbecue served from a long table set in the entrance of her mother's family home in the village of Caldearenas. Documents for the farmhouse trace its history back to the 17th century, but parts of the home are much older. The main building is a rambling construction in stone. Off to one side of the entrance is a stable for horses and the storage of firewood, hay and tools. From a small room at the other side of the entrance a door leads down to a large cellar where oils, grain and wine are kept. Across a small, fenced-in yard for hens and livestock is another barn for cows and oxen. All-year-round self-sufficiency was once an obligation for survival in remote country areas.

Exploring some of the out-buildings, we came across an old wooden sledge-like implement with rows of sharp stones embedded in the underside. Drawn behind a horse or donkey, this *trillo* was once used for threshing wheat. Together with a winnowing fork, wooden baskets formerly used in the fields during the grape harvest and an old cart, we had the wherewithal to begin farming again.

At the back of the building is a flour mill which operated until 1962, and which could easily be refurbished to its original condition. Blanca's grandfather, a village patriarch of considerable energy and imagination, had been responsible for diverting water to run a generator to provide both power to the mill and electricity for the village. He also organised the railway to come via the village en route from Zaragoza to Jaca. His energy and forceful personality did not always endear him to the rest of the village, and Blanca is sometimes sensitive to some lingering resentment. This is not evident in the small village bar, which will never shut while Blanca is still singing. She has a magnificent voice and an incredible repertoire of Spanish,

French and English songs, including a rendition of a *jota* that brings tears to the eye. I've never been convinced that by becoming a pharmacist she had made the correct career choice.

At lunch, Pete made a big hit with Blanca's mother. At seventy-odd, Maria-Dolores still retained the gaiety of a teenager. She didn't speak English and Pete had no Spanish, but a very few Japanese words served as the lingua franca. Pete was already beginning to display his ecumenical nature where by virtue of an uninhibited laugh and conspicuous good nature he could strike up a friendship almost instantly with anyone. Language skills — who needed them?

Blanca's father is a retired wine maker from Cariñena — the best-known wine area in Aragon. A gruff exterior and dismissive contempt of most wines conceals a heart of boundless generosity. He is a long-time favourite of my children: Sarah has fond memories of a visit to Zaragoza when Manolo rang up at 11.30 p.m. to invite the children out to an ice cream parlour.

'I'll pop around and pick you all up at 1 a.m.'

Sarah was ten years old at the time; José's children, aged four and eight, had school the next day. That the streets were still crowded with people at 1 a.m. was not in the least bit unusual and serves to illustrate the low priority the Spanish give to sleep.

The evening at José and Blanca's home in the centre of Zaragoza was devoted to conviviality, conversation and gastronomy — a splendid meal of Russian salad, an Asturian dish of clams cooked in white wine, and flan caramel. Pete tried several times to refuse third and fourth helpings by explaining how he was committed to losing weight.

'That's all very well,' said José, patting his own stomach, 'but I'm afraid that it is just not possible in Aragon!'

That evening we explored Zaragoza. According to the media and the politicians, Spain was in the grip of a serious economic depression. Official estimates of the rate of unemployment varied between 16 and 23 per cent, I'm not sure anyone knew the exact figure. However, even if the worst was true, it appeared that only the politicians and the media were depressed. In the bars, everyone else was enjoying themselves in the time-honoured fashion. The women were as elegant as ever, and the shops full of beautiful and unaffordable items. It is a pity that the rest of the world couldn't learn to be depressed like the Spanish.

*A*lmejas en Salsa Picante

Clams in a Spicy Sauce

There are many elegant seafood dishes to be experienced in Spain. This particular one which Blanca served is from Asturias in the north-west of Spain and is particularly well adapted to New Zealand conditions given our wonderful accessibility to pipis, tuatuas and clams on coastal beaches.

Ingredients:

1¹/₂ kg clams	2 good pinches
1 clove garlic	cayenne pepper (or a finely
¹/₂ cup olive oil	chopped chilli)
1 onion	1 fresh bay leaf
1 glass dry white wine	1 Tblsp flour
1 Tblsp paprika	1 handful fresh parsley

1. *In a large container soak shellfish in several changes of cold fresh water and salt over several hours to eliminate some of the sand.*
2. *In a large frying pan, gently fry the garlic clove in the olive oil until golden, being careful not to burn it. Remove the garlic, raise the heat, and fry the chopped onions until translucent. Add the shellfish and cover.*
3. *As soon as the shellfish begin to open, add the white wine, paprika, chilli pepper, bay leaf, and then sprinkle over the flour.*
4. *Allow to cook uncovered for about 5 minutes, stirring constantly to stop the flour sticking. Be careful — too much cooking will result in the shellfish becoming tough.*
5. *Sprinkle with chopped parsley and serve immediately.*

*I*dentity Crisis at Puente La Reina
June 10

A relaxing morning dedicated to catching up with mail, strolling at leisure around Zaragoza and exploring El Pilar, a huge church dedicated to the Virgin, who appeared to Saint James whilst he was evangelising in Spain. This event was the inspiration for many of the art works in the church, including paintings of Goya, who was born in a small village not far from here and who may have been in the city when Napoleon's troops breached the walls after a long and bitter siege. Exposure to the realities of war and its excesses of violence soured Goya's view of the French Revolution as heralding a new period of enlightenment in Europe. Such sensibilities would not prevent him from spending his twilight years in Bordeaux, but then as Pete and I had observed, France has other attractions besides political philosophy.

Returning from El Pilar, we wandered through the little squares that punctuate the old part of town. In these narrow streets, when walking off an evening meal that never starts before 10 p.m. and rarely finishes before midnight, José can be guaranteed to say, 'I know a place!'

This innocent phrase is a coded signal for the start of a round of bars of varied personalities, atmospheres and decors, each catering for an equally diverse range of clientele searching, alone or in any combination, for specialised tapas, hams, and different genres of music. José is blessed with that Hispanic constitution that attains peak form at 3 a.m., a time when only thieves and vagabonds are at large in New Zealand. Some people mistakenly attribute this phase lag of several hours between Spain and the rest of the world — lunch for example begins at 2 p.m. — to the institution of siesta. In my experience, there is more truth in José's gentle response to my young son, worried about where we would sleep after a very late arrival in Zaragoza: 'Don't worry. You know Sean, in Spain, we never sleep.'

That may have been true of Spaniards, but not Kiwis. Tonight we would sleep in a seminary in Puente La Reina — a town in Navarra where the many different routes from Europe to Santiago merge to form

El Camino — and from this point, restart our pilgrimage. José drove us there from Zaragoza and on arrival we were confronted with a surrealistic scene comprising several youngsters, all in training for priesthood, tormenting a rooster. On graduation, they would be able to torture entire congregations.

José had written a letter stating that we were 'serious' pilgrims from the Parish of Saint James, Kerikeri, New Zealand. And thus began a prelude to many similar conversations:

'*De donde?*' [From where?]

'*Nueva Zelanda.*'

'*Ah, Zelanda, Holandés?*' [Ah, Zeeland, Dutch?]

'*No, Neozelandés.*' [No, New Zealanders.]

'*Alemán?*' [German?]

'*No, no! Pacífico.*' [No, no! Pacific Ocean.]

'*Irlandés?*' [Irish?]

'*Montañas, grandes pescados,* sheep all over the bloody place, Kiri Te Kanawa, Zinzan Brooke.' [Mountains, big fish...]

'Disneyland, California?'

'*España*...dig big hole...New Zealand.'

'Woods Hole, Massachusetts?'

'First country to give women the vote!'

'*Heréticos!*' [Heretics!]

'*Antípodas.*' [Antipodes.]

'*Ah, Australianos, canguros!*' [Ah, Australians, kangaroos!]

'Close enough!'

After some further discussion we were granted a pilgrim's passport (*Credencial del Peregrino*), which, as in ancient times, would allow us to overnight in hostels or refuges along the route. A very modest donation (about $NZ5) entitled one to a mattress and, on occasions, a pillow. Expecting to sleep in fields along the route, we were heavily and unnecessarily overloaded with all the accoutrements of camping.

We left our packs at the seminary, and with José explored the narrow streets. In former times, this once-fortified town served to guard passage across the river Salado and to provide security from incursions by Moors. Puente La Reina (literally 'Bridge of the Queen') takes its name from a beautiful, multi-arched 11th century bridge built by a warrior queen, who almost lost her life crossing the Salado at this point.

We eventually settled upon a small family bar with a wonderful display of tapas including snails, kidneys in a sherry sauce, cockles and spicy sausages particular to this region of Navarra. After cigars and peach brandies, José, with some considerable reluctance, left to drive back to Zaragoza. A wonderful, generous friend with a remarkable sense of humour.

*R*iñones al Jerez
Kidneys in Sherry

As a student, I was once faced with having to divide a goat we had slaughtered amongst three friends — not an easy task given that using a binary model, God has designed most animals for easy division into two. The problem was resolved when my Ghanian friend announced that he was only interested in the internal anatomy — and the blood! After you've tried this dish and a haggis or two, you may think he got the best of the bargain.

Ingredients:

8 to 10 lamb's kidneys
1 Tblsp wine vinegar
2 Tblsp olive oil
1 onion, finely chopped
1 clove garlic, crushed
1 tsp paprika
2 Tblsp fresh breadcrumbs
1 tsp dried oregano
1 bay leaf

4 to 6 Tblsp dry sherry (Cognac is a good substitute — Madeira and port are also fine as long as you add a teaspoon of mustard to counteract some of the sweetness)
150 ml water
salt and pepper
fresh parsley

1. *Slice kidneys thinly and remove the membranes and gristly bits. Leave to soak in water and vinegar for several hours.*
2. *Heat oil in a heavy pan. Fry onion and garlic with a little salt until they go limp. Add the kidneys and toss in the hot oil for a minute or two.*
3. *Stir in the paprika, breadcrumbs and herbs. Pour in the sherry and bubble vigorously to evaporate off the alcohol.*
4. *Add the water and bring to the boil. Cover tightly and turn down the heat. Simmer gently for 15–20 minutes until kidneys are tender and the sauce thick and rich. Salt and pepper to taste, and then sprinkle with chopped parsley.*
5. *Serve hot.*

*E*stella

June 11

*W*e spent a relatively uneventful but pleasant day ambling through an almost Mediterranean landscape — olives, grapes, cereals, asparagus, and a juxtaposition of irrigated crops and fallow fields. A rainbow of wild flowers lined the route. While I was not insensitive to this infusion of nature, readers will learn little of local botany from this epistle as I'm woefully ignorant of the names of flowers. For this knowledge lack, I blame a primary school teacher who forced me at an impressionable age to enter a flower-arranging competition. I had made no secret of my loathing for anything remotely concerned with gardening, and had duly arrived at school without any flowers. Refusing to listen to reason, this paradigm of authoritarianism ordered me home with strict instructions not to return empty-handed.

And so I had not, but only after first seething with indignation all the way home and then venting my rage upon my mother's garden, furiously pulling out entire plants at random. My final act of rebellion had been to throw the flowers — or weeds — that had survived the walk back to school haphazardly into the only vase remaining.

'That will teach her,' or so I thought.

I was awarded first prize — with a special commendation for my 'imaginative arrangement and flamboyant use of colour'.

On entry to Estella we walked past the ruins of the Church of the Holy Sepulchre and its Gothic facade with beautiful statues of the twelve Apostles, and then on through a neighbourhood or *barrio* once settled by Jews expelled from Castilla in 1492. From here, they would be subsequently expelled once again in the 14th century during the Inquisition. In the Middle Ages, when the church still retained the high moral ground on all ethical and sociological questions, usury was considered on a par with adultery. To have aspirations beyond one's God-given station was a risky business: money-lenders came in for a particularly tough time — usurers could not be admitted to communion and were refused Christian burial. Denied the opportunity to own land, the Jews of the Diaspora had little choice but to engage in such dubious activities and duly suffered society's disapprobation.

Estella occupied a natural link between the sheep farmers of the north and the cropping areas to the south. It has long been a market town, its importance assured in the 11th century when successive Kings of Aragon and Pamplona ordered that the road to Santiago should pass through the region and granted special privileges to the Frankish populations already settled there. By the 14th century, it is said that the town was so strongly French that they spoke Provençal.

Most of the architecturally important monuments are to be found in the French quarter, including the church of San Pedro de la Rua, where we sat amongst a small congregation of elderly women. The church itself was mainly Gothic in style, but had some lovely light Romanesque chapels and a cloister which has been half-destroyed since the 16th century, when the fortress on the rock behind the church collapsed and fell upon it. Clearly not the rock of salvation.

Church architecture was still a bit of a mystery and we felt quite naive amongst such wonderful art works. Nevertheless, the atmosphere was reverent and conducive to prayer. We remembered our families and our many friends who had helped us thus far.

It was Saturday evening and time for tapas. The Plaza de San Miguel was full of families *tomando el fresco* (taking the air) with their young children. Teenagers chatted animatedly in bars whilst other groups basked in the evening sun around tables on the square. A troupe of Gipsies tuned up and then moved off for a performance elsewhere. The quintessence of Spain.

*P*iperrada

Mountain ranges in Europe serve neither as linguistic nor culinary barriers and this wonderful breakfast, lunch or dinner dish is common to the Basque provinces on either side of the Pyrénées.

Ingredients:

2 medium-sized onions	a good pinch of cayenne pepper
2 large sweet peppers	or several drops of Tabasco sauce
3 to 4 Tblsp olive oil	salt and pepper
1 branch of thyme	6 eggs
1 bay leaf	1 Tblsp chopped parsley
1 clove garlic	butter for frying
2 large tomatoes	4 rashers grilled bacon

1. *Brown sliced onions and peppers in olive oil with the thyme, bay leaf, and an intact clove of garlic. Cover and leave cooking slowly for 10 minutes.*

2. *Add the tomatoes, sliced and peeled, cayenne pepper or Tabasco sauce, and salt and pepper to taste. Cook gently for a further 20 minutes or so in order to obtain an oily mixture. Remove the garlic, thyme and bay leaf.*

3. *While the above mixture is simmering, beat the eggs. Sprinkle with salt and pepper, and mix in the parsley.*

4. *Heat the butter and a little olive oil in a saucepan with a heavy base. Toss in the beaten egg mixture.*

5. *Cook over a gentle heat until the omelette just begins to set and then stir in the tomato and capsicum mixture with a fork. The combination should be soft and velvety.*

6. *Serve garnished with slices of grilled bacon. (Most recipes in France and Spain use a dark, smoked ham with a quite different taste from that to which we are more accustomed. However, one can rarely come to grief by substituting one for the other.)*

Variation: *We often make just an ordinary omelette and garnish it with the piperrada preparation rather than scrambling it into the eggs.*

*Є*stella to Los Arcos
June 12

*T*he guidebook implied that today was to be a short (22 kilometre) walk to Los Arcos without a lot of interest on route. Our first adventure was our now habitual breakfast of *café con leche* (coffee with milk) together with a couple of *magdalenas* (not repentant prostitutes, in this case, but small cakes reminiscent of English Madeira cake). Tame really, compared with other clients getting kick-started with a tonic comprising two-thirds of a cup of brandy, one or two teaspoons of sugar, and a mint leaf, clove, or aniseed flower for flavouring. This high explosive was ignited, left until the flaming mixture had caramelised, and then doused with coffee. Drunk with a glass of red wine, this was a concoction guaranteed to overcome any touch of the humours.

The *café con leche* got us through to the monastery of Irache, with its splendid assemblage of old carts in the covered-in portion of the cloister. This collection, and other undoubted architectural splendours of the church and associated buildings, once housed the first hospital in Navarra (dating from 1050), and would have received more critical examination if it had not been for a more beguiling treasure, the Bodega de Irache and its pilgrim fountain. Nothing unusual about a fountain; we had enjoyed several already, but none that had offered a choice of water or wine!

Some choice. There were instructions for pilgrims not to

abuse this fresh, delectable *clarete*, but they were in Spanish and so held no particular relevance or reverence for us and thus it was not until some considerable time later that we were able to resume our quest. The ambience was once again very Mediterranean. Wild flowers lined the path and the air was steeped with the fragrance of native aromatic

herbs. Rocks and herbs gave a bluish tinge to the sunlit arid slopes, whilst a shepherd, crossing the path ahead with his herd of sheep and goats, contributed the finishing touches to this biblical pastiche.

Drunk on these rural vistas so different from the pastoral farming and wild virginal forest scenes of our homeland, our perambulations were rudely interrupted by the appearance of an old man on a motorbike who, after some linguistic difficulties, convinced us that we had just walked 6 kilometres in the wrong direction. We understood what he was saying but just didn't want to believe him. What a catastrophe! A march of more than one hour, assuming that one could maintain a steady course.

This backtracking was to prove timely as our eventual arrival in Arqueta coincided with a Basque religious festival. The entire village population was in the act of abandoning the church and making its way towards the bar. Outside stood a small statue of the Virgin adorned with flowers. We were invited to join them, and indeed, it would have been churlish to refuse. That not a soul spoke English or French, or even Japanese, proved no handicap to conversation. Our mouths stuffed with local cheeses, salami and red wine, the odd gesture, often very odd, proved to be a sufficient contribution to the dialogue. Pete drew a map of the world and convinced them that we were from Australia.

Conscious that our progress today had not been spectacular, we tried unsuccessfully to refuse successive glasses of wine, but that was obviously considered quite antisocial and as representatives of the New World, we were anxious not to offend.

'This wine is made without chemicals. Completely natural!'

'Without water, you mean?'

'Of course!'

At some point we extricated ourselves from this almost overwhelming hospitality, after promising to pray for Anna, Condida, and Margarita in Santiago. And to think that in the 12th century, one pilgrim, an Amery Picaud, had accused these Navarrese of all sorts of perfidy and outrageous crimes, including fornicating with mules. Difficult to believe — perhaps the real problem was Picaud. As my son once said of his teacher after having been accused yet again of disrupting the class: 'He's got an attitude problem!'

Whatever else may have changed since the Middle Ages, the ancient custom of granting hospitality to pilgrims had obviously still survived through to modern times.

I'm sure that the remainder of the route was at least as beautiful as the earlier portion, but at the time of writing it is difficult to bring it clearly to mind. Moreover, my diary is quite difficult to read. We would have done well to remember the chronicle of one Jean Froissart describing the arrival in Santiago de Compostela in 1386 of John of Gaunt with his English troops and retinue.

> *They found there flesshe and strong wyne ynough, wherof the Englysshe archers dranke so moche that they were ofte tymes dronken, wherby they had fevers, orelles in the mornyng theyr hedes were so evyl, that they coulde not helpe themselfe all the day after...*[4]

Well, we were at least still walking and in a particularly relaxed frame of mind. Somehow we arrived in Los Arcos. This was another place settled by French merchants and also called in the Middle Ages 'the Jewish Town'. Today everything, including the church, was closed and the accommodation rather insalubrious. In fact, it wasn't a hostel for pilgrims but rather a place where visitors having nowhere else to stay could spend the odd night — a rather nice concept. Pete wanted to continue.

At Torres del Rio we went searching for a light snack. The village seemed deserted. It transpired that everyone was in the bar watching the Spanish soccer cup final. One television per village is a particularly attractive concept and what better place to locate it? After a couple of shandies and tuna in a vinaigrette sauce, we shambled a discrete distance out of town and pitched the tent in a wheat field.

I spent most of the night listening to Pete snore. In principle, I don't object to snoring, but I just hate anyone sleeping when I can't.

A very uneventful day, indeed.

*C*hilindrón de Cordero

Lamb Stewed with Peppers

Lamb is superb in this part of the world and so are the peppers. This dish, common to Navarra and Aragon, combines the best of both.

Ingredients:

5 or 6 Tblsp olive oil	2 big, ripe tomatoes
3 cloves garlic	4 to 6 red peppers
1½ kg lamb shoulder-meat, cut into cubes	2 Tblsp chopped parsley
	1 bay leaf
salt and freshly ground black pepper	2 tsp paprika
	1 good pinch cayenne pepper
2 onions, chopped	salt and pepper

1. *Heat half of the oil in a flameproof casserole and gently fry the cloves of garlic until golden, being careful not to burn them. Add half of the lamb and fry over a high heat until browned on all sides. Season and remove from pan. Brown the rest of the meat in the same manner. Set the meat to one side.*

2. *Add more oil if needed and fry the onions. Chop the tomatoes and slice the peppers and then add with the herbs and spices. Continue to cook for a few minutes, season with salt and pepper and then return the lamb to the dish.*

3. *Cover tightly and simmer for 1 hour over a very low heat. The tomatoes should release enough liquid to make a good sauce, but check periodically that it isn't drying out. If that is the case, lower the heat and moisten with a little water or dry white wine.*

4. *Before serving, check the seasoning — it should be spicy because of the paprika and cayenne.*

$\mathcal{A}$lone to Logroño

June 13

$\mathcal{W}$e had stopped in Viana for a drink. When asked to fill up our water bottle, the barman pointed to the village fountain on the square, and replied: 'The water there is better and colder, pilgrims have been using it for centuries.'

In the Pyrénées, we had been circumspect about drinking from streams or village sources because of still-vivid memories of a violent bout of diarrhoea incurred during an earlier visit to an idyllic little village so high up in the French Basque country that a contaminated water supply seemed inconceivable. Pete and I were not averse to losing weight, but not all at once. But henceforth, we would throw caution to the wind and sup directly from village fountains. Why argue with tradition?

Pete had decided that he would catch the bus to Logroño and buy a better pair of boots. Many times we had rued the advice of 'experts'. Rather than equipping ourselves for a mountain-climbing expedition in the Himalayas, we should have come armed with a light pair of running shoes. Pete now had so many blisters on his feet that he ruefully exclaimed, 'It's like walking with hydrolastic suspension.'

It was remarkable that he had been able to make it this far. But at least it was marginally better than some penitents and criminals in the Middle Ages, condemned by the Inquisition to voyage bare-footed or hobbled with ankle chains until they rusted through.

Leaving Viana and its ancient streets, I plodded on alone towards Logroño. The last part of the route was an environmental disaster — polluted waterways, marginals in makeshift housing, scrap metal dealers, junk collectors, and very friendly people.

Stemming from days when towns had to be fortified, and the need to be close to a source of water, Spanish towns are surprisingly confined. No amber lights, no diffuse boundary of Legoland houses, sprinkled lawns, and clipped hedges: at one moment, you are clearly in the countryside and then within a few steps, you find yourself in town. In ancient times, the exterior of the town was where all the rubbish was dumped, and in Logroño, this tradition continues to the present day.

I entered Logroño by way of the old stone bridge crossing the river, and, as the refuge had not yet opened, made my way to the town centre where I was completely unprepared for the beauty of the inner city squares, parks and fountains. No greater contrast with the somewhat sordid entry could be imagined.

It was late afternoon and the squares were bursting with young mothers, grandmothers and children. Later they would participate in the national sport of doing a round of the bars and enjoying tapas with friends and relatives. I got in some early practice sampling a few seafood canapés, and then after a substantive communion of a couple of glasses of superb Rioja, that rich, full-bodied, oaky red wine for which the region is famous, found a church for some moments of reflection and Bible study. Having cracked Genesis, I was now on to Deuteronomy. Gripping stuff! But as with *El Camino*, there was more of the Bible in front of me than behind.

Leaving the intricacies of Mosaic Law for the Rabbis, I explorambled around Logroño, discovering by accident the portal of the Church of Santiago del Real, with its baroque representation of Santiago-Matamoros — Saint James the Moorkiller — resplendent in cape and sabre, mounted on a huge horse scattering the Saracen foe. Today it is easy to forget the shock waves that the discovery of the tomb of Saint James sent through Christian Europe. This was a time when Islam was in ascendancy: Cordoba had the greatest mosque in the world, and Arab thinkers were making great advances in mathematics and astronomy. In Logroño we were only a few kilometres from Albelda de Irega, where the Arab numerical system was introduced into Europe and which, through the use of the zero and the decimal system, allowed for the more rapid development of mathematics. The discovery of the tomb of Saint James, one of Christ's original apostles — who had witnessed the Transfiguration and the risen Christ — provided a new focus for Christendom and one which would lead to the eventual reconquest of the entire Iberian peninsula. Saint James the Apostle became Saint James the Slayer of Moors, and according to mythology whenever the Spanish forces were at their lowest ebb, Saint James would appear on horseback turning certain defeat into devastating victory. This tradition has continued with 'Santiago' becoming the battle cry of the Spanish Armed Forces.

Meanwhile, Pete had managed to find the refuge. It was new and very tastefully constructed with a modern kitchen, hot showers and a lovely courtyard with barbecue facilities. Except for the communal sleeping arrangements, it could have been a hotel. We rested for a while and then it was time to celebrate and drink to family and absent friends. Some other pilgrims, whom we would get to know very well in the forthcoming weeks, suggested a modest restaurant opposite the bullring with a menu featuring typical regional dishes. And celebrate we did with *sopa de pescado*, followed by grilled lamb chops, French fries, and red peppers, two bottles of the 12-year-old house wine, chocolate ice-cream, coffee, and brandy and cigars on the house. Ooh, the life of a pilgrim is rough.

After an evening of such unrepentant self-indulgence, the reader may well have expected me to dwell on the vexed question of whether gluttony was, or was not, one of the cardinal sins. Didn't it say somewhere: 'There are six things the Lord hates, seven that are detestable to him...'?

But did that list include gormandise? Could sin be prioritised? and if so was gluttony a lesser sin than adultery? Sex! Celibacy! Adultery! Castration! Where did the curious attitude of the church towards celibacy in the priesthood originate? The first Pope was married — well Peter at least had a mother-in-law. Intriguing questions; subjects worthy of lengthy consideration, serious examination, and in the fullness of time, open debate.

'Good questions, John! Well asked!' said the self-conscious me. 'Just leave them to me.'

'Whew!' replied the other me, as it fell immediately into a deep, dreamless sleep.

ꟻopa de Pescado
Fish Soup

Originating as a simple fisherman's dish made from the day's catch and locally available vegetables, fish soup is common in both France and Spain. The flavour is more interesting if as many different varieties as possible of fish, crabs, and/or shellfish are included. It can be strained and served directly as an entrée, thickened with pasta for a more substantial main course, or, as is the case with the best known of all fish soups, the bouillabaisse from Marseille, embellished with a spicy, garlic-flavoured mayonnaise sauce (alioli).

Ingredients:

2 onions, finely chopped
1 leek, chopped
¹/₂ cup olive oil
4 cloves of garlic, mashed
500 g ripe tomatoes
1¹/₂ litres water (or 750 ml of water and
   the same quantity of dry white wine)
1¹/₂ kg assorted whole fish, fish heads, bones and
   trimmings, and, if available, shellfish
1 bouquet garni composed of parsley, thyme, bay leaf
1 tsp saffron powder
1 Tblsp finely chopped parsley
salt and freshly ground pepper

1. *Cook onions and leek slowly in several tablespoons of the olive oil for 5 or so minutes until the onions are translucent.*
2. *Stir in garlic and tomatoes and cook for a further 5 minutes.*
3. *In a large tureen or pot add the rest of the olive oil, water and wine, fish, herbs and seasonings; boil gently uncovered for 30 to 40 minutes.*
4. *Strain through a coarse sieve, pressing the juice out of the ingredients.*

5. *At this point there are several options. You may either:*
   (a) add shellfish in their shells to the liquid, cook for a further 10 minutes and then serve immediately after correcting the seasoning, or,
   (b) add ¹/₂ cup of pasta and boil for a further 12 to 15 minutes until tender. Correct seasoning, and serve, or,
   (c) if you really want to impress, pour the soup into bowls over bread rounds, and serve separately with grated parmesan cheese and alioli (see page 55).

*T*o Sleep, Perchance to Dream

June 14

*R*ather than plunge directly back into the fray, Pete went by bus to allow his blisters one more day to heal while I trudged on alone. The guidebook waxed lyrical about the beauties of Navarrete, but today it seemed without charm and inhabited by surly people; a collection of mud-coloured houses on the side of a hill. Perhaps I was just out of sorts after having to walk on the main highway and to continually avoid oncoming trucks. At one point I had decided to walk on the other side of the road — that way you didn't see what was about to kill you. Better still, the turbulence in wakes of passing trucks blew from behind, giving one a gentle nudge in the right direction rather than violently knocking you sideways and blowing off your hat. The Traffic Patrol of the Guardia Civil, disinterested in debating the finer details of fluid mechanics, ordered me to cross back and face the music.

On my arrival in Nájera, Pete was resting by the river. He had promised to use the time profitably to learn a few critical words of Spanish starting with, '*La cuenta, por favor*' [Can I have the bill, please?].

Too shrewd to fall for that cheap ruse, Pete had already managed to lose my wife's phrase book. Well, one had to admit that Pete's natural bonhomie was proving a more than adequate substitute for conversation.

Waiting for the monastery to open, we both fell asleep on a bench in the town square, oblivious to its wonderful history. According to legend, it was here in 1044 whilst falconing that the king observed his hawk follow a dove down into a grotto. In pursuit of the falcon, the king eventually found both birds sitting peacefully together before a statue of the Virgin. Above this grotto, the monastery now houses the sepulchre of one of the queens of Navarra, as well as many tombs of knights. The wonderful detail of the queen's sculptured marble coffin miraculously escaped the fate of many of the other art works in the church during the Wars of Independence. Although guide books seldom mention them, I found the carved wooden doors and choirs here, as in many other churches, simply remarkable. Anyone who has attempted even a minimal amount of woodwork would not fail to recognise the impossibility of such artistry.

Our siesta successfully completed, Pete and I strolled around the old streets trying a variety of tapas including all those wonderful internal parts of animals, such as sweetbreads, kidneys, tripe and brains, now frowned upon by modern Anglo-Saxon cuisine. Recipe books from our grandparents' time sometimes hold more interest than contemporary tomes, with their preoccupation with speed, health and longevity. We seem to be breeding a generation of people squeamishly artificial and boring in their dietary aspirations. When the occasion permits, I take pleasure in hunting, and once, after a succession of evening meals like possum soup, jugged hare and roast kid of goat, my son complained, 'Why do we always have to eat home-made meat?'

It isn't that Sean doesn't enjoy such dishes, but rather is embarrassed when his friends 'get wind' of our deviant preferences. (To digress for just a brief instant, it is actually a very sensible precaution to always eat wild goat upwind of other guests.) However, the point is that if we are not careful, sanitary considerations will become the sole culinary criterion, and taste irrelevant. Despite the increasing sophistication of kitchens, people today seem less and less interested in cooking — Japanese technology and Anglo-Saxon aspirations.

But thank goodness for the French and Spanish! In one of many studies searching for links between diet and the incidence of heart disease, statistics from agricultural workers in the south and north of France, Wales and Scotland, were compared. By carefully eliminating other socio-economic factors, this particular study aimed to narrow in on dietary and a few other lifestyle considerations. The south of France came out clearly as having the lowest incidence of coronary problems, a fact often attributed to the consumption of red wine, olive oil and garlic. Alioli is a splendid example of a dish that combines all the merits of the latter two ingredients, and will come as surprise to those who have only used commercial mayonnaise — try it with squid rings or salted fish, and boiled potatoes with a light sprinkling of cayenne pepper. But to return to the original argument (it is hard to talk for too long about the merits of food without getting distracted by the real thing), the varied nature of the Mediterranean diet, high quality ingredients, a balance between fresh vegetables and meat, an inherited interest in food, and never listening to American doctors, must all contribute to this medical mystery.

The wine hypothesis certainly needed further testing and Pete and I, ever ready to sacrifice our health for the common good, were prepared to dedicate our livers to this cause. Benedictine monks were allowed a quarter litre of wine a day if total abstinence was not possible. Walking as well as praying, abstinence was simply not an option.

We entered a shop selling berets. By now it had already become very clear that Pete was very 'ethnic'. Everywhere, people assumed he was Spanish — perhaps not from this region exactly but probably from the neighbouring province. A beret would complement this ethnicity, completing his disguise so as to be indistinguishable from a Basque farmer. Alas, the Philistine was not interested, concerned only that it would be one more thing to carry. If I'd suggested another kilogram of *confit de canard*, he may have been more excited. After 30 minutes of wasted argument, it was I who emerged wearing the beret — an Irish Basque?

Next door was a jewellery shop, and since all day I had been getting little paraphysical reminders from my wife of my promise to buy her a watch, we carefully examined the possibilities in the window. Pete pointed to one that Delphine would have adored. It was exquisite and probably solid gold. Well, why not — isn't it right and proper to spoil your loved ones?

'How much?'

'$2000 American.'

Ouch! I should have known — whenever prices were quoted in American dollars, it was a clear signal that only Americans could afford them.

'I wonder how much a watch that she wouldn't like would cost?'

That night sleep evaded us both. The cause: two elderly American priests, who had arrived late, heavily overladen even by our standards. We had felt sorry for them. This charity didn't extend through the night, however, as with their snoring they explored new extremes of the decibel scale. What a racket! Would it be possible to carry them both carefully to the cathedral without waking them and just leave them there? The resonance caused by their seismic sibilations would have surely destroyed the 500-year-old roof and put an end to our problem.

'Not a very Christian thought, John,' said God, reading my mind.

'But a damn good one,' says I.

'Hmmm!'

In the morning, I repented these villainous but immensely comforting thoughts. The cloister presented an atmosphere of complete peace and serenity. God seemed very close and I commended my family and friends to His protection. Perhaps I should talk to Him more often.

$\mathcal{A}$lioli
Aïoli

A strongly aromatic mayonnaise sauce flavoured with garlic, alioli can be served with many dishes such as poached fish, boiled potatoes, snails, deep-fried calamari, or as a flavoursome dip for fresh vegetables. If you make this to accompany fish soup serve it in a separate dish; each guest helps himself and stirs it into the soup with a liberal quantity of grated Parmesan cheese.

The Provençal poet, Fréderic Mistral (1891) said of aïoli that 'it concentrates within us, the heat, the strength and the jubilation of the Provençal sun...; it also has another virtue: it chases away the flies.'

Warning! According to a French newspaper, don't attempt to make aïoli on the night of a full moon — it will never work properly!

Ingredients:

6 cloves mashed garlic	1 tsp thyme
a pinch of salt	2 egg yolks (as with the potato
1 medium-sized cooked and	these must be at room
cooled potato	temperature)
1 tsp basil	4 to 6 Tblsp olive oil

1. *Crush the garlic in a mortar with a pinch of salt.*
2. *Pound the potato and herbs in with the crushed garlic.*
3. *Beat in the egg yolks to form a sticky paste.*
4. *Stirring constantly, beat in the olive oil, drop by drop at first as if making a mayonnaise: it is imperative that the oil be added very slowly initially until the sauce begins to thicken. After this, the oil may be incorporated a little more quickly.*

Variation: *To make the alioli into a rouille add ¼ cup of crushed red peppers and a few drops of Tabasco sauce to the potato, herb and garlic mixture. Then add the egg yolk and olive oil as above. A little tomato paste and a pinch of saffron might be tolerated at this point but are not essential.*

*S*anto Domingo de la Calzada

June 15

*I*n Azofra, after stopping to buy some oranges and yogurt for lunch, we were accosted by an elderly woman who insisted that we follow her to visit the refuge and the church. She was clearly very proud of them both. The refuge was brand new, with hot showers. Why hadn't we stayed here last night? Our hostess made us a fresh cup of coffee before stamping our pilgrim's passports with great care and deliberation. She then took us on a tour of the small church which she opened with a gigantic key. The church was beautiful in its simplicity, and its prize piece was a 14th century figurine of the crucifixion. After talking with her, I'd again adopted Australian citizenship — New Zealand was just too complicated to explain.

On the outskirts of the village we passed an old man with a scythe heading out into the fields. Pointing out the fountain for the pilgrims, he insisted that we sample a more sustaining liquid — this year's vintage. It was wonderful — fruity, not too alcoholic, an ideal breakfast beverage!

By midday the sun was merciless, and it was with some relief that we at last arrived in Santo Domingo. We showered in the refuge, which we guessed had been, in ancient times, a hospital for pilgrims. It is a fabulous building with a cobblestoned entrance and a winding narrow staircase leading up to the pilgrims' quarters. And cool! Recovering from the rigours of the morning's march in the depths of two old, scarred leather armchairs, relics of a more gracious age, we gazed at the massive blackened beams and white plastered ceilings. It was now time to eat, and with some effort we surfaced from several fathoms of leather, struggled to our feet and went out in search of a nice restaurant, which we found without much difficulty.

The waitress was absolutely stunning and Pete could scarcely believe his eyes. The daily routine of exercise must have damaged my hormone levels to the point where I was curiously unaffected by proximity to such beauty — I just needed food. While she explained the menu of the day, Pete became more and more oblivious to my rough but immensely clever simultaneous translations. I ceased to exist as he just said '*sí*' or '*no*' completely at random, but always with the firm conviction that he was communicating directly with this delectable young maiden on some higher, ethereal plane. At the choice of the desserts, the waitress, determined to display her linguistic talents, said, instead of '*manzana*', 'apple' in English. Pete turned to me, as if struck by a bomb, almost shouting, 'Apple! Apple! What's "apple"?'

Back in the refuge, we were just treading time again in those leather armchairs when our two American colleagues emerged from a nap. They must have arrived while we were eating; pretty good going considering their age and how they had looked yesterday. Perhaps they had cowardly avoided wine at breakfast. Awake, one of our adenoidal friends turned out to have spent most of his life in South America. They were Jesuits. I was curious about this Order. Apparently it was begun in 1533 by Ignatius Loyola, who had been born in Naverrete, through which I had passed yesterday en route to Nájera. Originally a soldier, Loyola was wounded by a cannonball in a battle near Pamplona, experienced a dramatic conversion, and subsequently founded the religious order.

My ears were still ringing from our friend's snoring during the night, and so it was with rather bad grace that I asked him why the Jesuits had often been so distrusted in former times.

'It is true that we were often accused of being clever, cunning and political,' he replied. 'This stems from our early history when the Jesuits became the Catholic church's main weapon against the Reformation and responsible for rooting out Protestant heresies. Eventually the

Order had become so powerful that it was disliked as much by Catholics as Protestants.'

He was right: the *Concise Oxford Dictionary* defines 'jesuitical' as 'equivocating' — and I thought their former unpopularity was only due to their snoring.

Jesuit ministries were also very vigorous abroad, particularly in South America where they raised the ire of the white colonists by preventing exploitation of the Indians. Because of this they found themselves under threat by both the Catholic church and the colonists. This persecution of the Jesuits continues today in the Honduras, where recent governments regard as suspicious the conversion of peasants, and subversive, the Catholic church's support for agrarian reform.

'The government is more tolerant of some new charismatic churches who encourage peasants to just concentrate on their relationship with God and to accept their unfortunate circumstances as all part of God's big plan. Their reward will come later in heaven.'

I too had difficulties with the concept that repressive governments are all part of God's plan — Jesus stressed spiritual priorities and the need to put one's relationship with God before earthly pursuits, but not a passive acceptance of injustice.

The priest also told us about the Benedictine Order whose monasteries we had seen and who had always put a strong emphasis on agriculture.

'With no central government, people often gave the first fruits of the harvest to the church. As a result of their own industry and gifts from the populace, monasteries sometimes became very wealthy, a circumstance quite at variance with the philosophy of poverty under which these Orders were originally established.'

I began to regret thinking such horrible things last night, but when asked if we were planning to stay here tonight, Pete and I replied in unison.

'No!'

There are limits to human forgiveness.

We visited the 12th century cathedral and the shrine of Santo Domingo, who had been responsible for building many of the roads and bridges en route to Santiago. In the 11th century there were many forests and few roads. According to history, Santo Domingo became a hermit after being rejected by the Benedictine Order and settled by the pilgrim road in the forest, where travellers were most at risk from bandits and wolves. There he built a chapel. After completing the causeway between Nájera and Redecilla, he constructed a hospital nearby, personally attending to pilgrims. Around this hospital grew the town which later took from the Saint its name, Santo Domingo de la Calzada.

The cathedral, which still maintains some vestiges of the original construction by the Saint, was one of the first Gothic churches in Spain. In addition to the shrine of Santo Domingo, it is celebrated for a miracle that allegedly took place in the town. One version of this story has it that the daughter of an innkeeper had cast her lecherous eye on the son of a German family travelling to Santiago. When her amorous advances were refused, she took revenge by placing a silver cup in his knapsack, and then raising the alarm of its theft just as the family were about to leave. The son was arrested, summarily tried and hanged. The rest of the family, a little disconsolate at this unexpected turn of events, continued on their pilgrimage, praying to Saint James for the soul of their son.

Upon their return some six weeks later, the family were amazed to find their son still hanging there, miraculously still alive and complaining of a sore neck. On being informed, the local magistrate was incredulous and not a little irritated at having his meal interrupted by such arrant nonsense.

'That young man has as much chance of still being alive as have these two roasted chickens.'

No sooner had these words been uttered when the two roast chickens jumped up and began to crow. And so it is to this day that a cock and hen are to be found caged in the church.

Still feeling quite fresh, Pete and I decided to carry on another 14 or so kilometres to

Redecilla del Camino. With any luck, we should be out of earshot of our Jesuit friends by nightfall.

The hostel in Redecilla del Camino was one of several old terraced homes lining the main route. It was still under reconstruction but comfortable enough once we had scavenged a few bits of styrofoam to serve as mattresses. We shared a room with a father and daughter from Galicia. In the adjacent chamber were two rather unsavoury characters, one of whom would become an all too familiar sight over the next week. I decided to call him Pancho.

$\mathcal{P}$oulet Roti Farci
Roast Stuffed Chicken

Extensive historical research in the Vatican archives (since destroyed) has revealed that this was the very dish prepared for the magistrate upon being told of the miraculous survival of the young man.

Ingredients:

For the stuffing:
1 chicken liver
a handful of bread moistened
   with a cup of milk
100 g ham
several spring onions
1 small onion
1/2 clove garlic
1 Tblsp chopped parsley
salt and pepper
1 egg
blood of the chicken

For the meat:
1 young roasting chicken
   (clearly dead but otherwise
   in peak condition)
750 ml good chicken stock
3 or 4 Tblsp olive oil
6 to 8 potatoes in their jackets

For the sauce:
1/2 cup wine vinegar
1 Tblsp finely chopped shallots
   or spring onion
chopped parsley
salt and pepper

1. *Make a stuffing using the minced liver, the moistened breadcrumbs, ham, onions, garlic, parsley, salt and pepper. Mince the mixture finely and thicken with a whole egg and as much as possible of the blood of the chicken. Salt the cavity and then stuff the chicken. Truss.*
2. *Brown the bird in olive oil. Season with salt and pepper. Place the chicken in an oven tray with enough stock to cover the base to a depth of 2–3 cm and then place the tray in the middle of a very hot oven. Count on a cooking time of about 25 minutes for each kilogram of meat. Baste the fowl frequently with liberal quantities of stock. Add more if necessary.*
3. *Meanwhile par-boil some whole potatoes in their jackets. Don't cook them until they go soft — the final cooking must take place in the oven. About*

20 minutes before completion, sit the potatoes around the chicken in the stock so that they can absorb the flavour of the juices while finishing their cooking.

4. *Serve directly from the cooking pan with the whole potatoes surrounding the chicken. Alternatively, purée the potatoes and season lightly; serve the chicken on a bed of purée. Before eating, pour some of the bouillon over the mashed potatoes and then dribble on a piquant sauce made by steeping finely chopped shallots or spring onions, salt and parsley in vinegar.*

$\mathscr{T}$he Mountains of Oca
June 16

$\mathscr{I}$n Beldorado I rested in the square, contemplating the impossibility of absolute rest in a universe with no absolute frame of reference. No wonder I was tired. Pete, meanwhile, struck up an acquaintance with the local pharmacist, buying several more kilograms of specialist plasters to add to his already considerable first-aid kit. His new boots were performing well, but the original blisters had still not healed.

Later that morning in Villafranca-de-Oca, I was given the run around by a young barman who affected vexation and irritation when asked for a drink of water. This was the first time that I had ever experienced communication difficulties in a bar — anywhere. Actually, that is a bit of an exaggeration; I once spent several weeks in a hotel in a small village near Albacete, south of Madrid. Each time, when asked if I could use the toilet behind the bar, the barman would answer '*sí*' and pour me a beer. When told this story, a friend in New Zealand had replied, 'Anyone else would have asked for a beer and been directed to the toilet.'

A pleasant young student helping out with the Camino found a key and let us into the church. We remarked that there seemed to be hardly any young people left in the villages. She explained, 'There are now so few jobs in the countryside that we have little choice but to leave our families for the city.'

The permanent population of Villafranca numbered about 100, of which the majority were elderly. This exodus to the cities is an inevitable consequence of modern technology and is exacerbated by agricultural policies which subsidise production. These subsidies encourage bigger farms, heavier machinery, and less and less people.

The ascent of the mountains of Oca began as we left the village. For pilgrims of former times, these bandit- and wolf-infested mountains were the ultimate test between the 'savage Navarra' and the 'welcoming Castilla'. Today they didn't seem in the least inhibiting — more like gentle hills. The first portion of the route was delightful as the path wound through alternating oak forest and small meadows. The light quality was lovely, with the muted hues amongst the trees contrasting with late-afternoon pastel colours of the meadows.

A little later and we were lost. We came upon a shepherd's shelter guarded by dogs who made it clear that we were not welcome. The shepherd would have grazing rights amongst small parcels of land allocated around the village. The absence of fences means that the small

flocks of 50 to 100 sheep and a few goats must be watched during the day and kept under shelter at night. The shepherd was nowhere to be seen.

After retracing our steps a kilometre or so, we found the path and continued climbing. On the hilltops, with the forest largely destroyed by fire, the landscape was desolate, depressing, and the path, endless. Vague, mostly forgotten memories of half-understood lectures on Einstein's theories floated through my head. I wished they would go away, but they kept turning up like a dog with bone. Undirected thought is probably very beneficial for the psyche, but today it seemed as if my brain was free-wheeling out of control and worrying about concepts that were far too difficult for it. Could the universe be bounded and at the same time be infinite? Certainly it would be possible to trace an infinite line on the surface of a sphere, and it was possible that Pete and I were in the process of proving just that. We rested more often but rigor mortis threatened and it became more and more difficult to restart. We were beginning to have considerably more sympathy with pilgrims of former times.

It was hellishly hot and we were both sweating so much that it was impossible to see through our sunglasses. Another perplexing physics phenomenon presented itself. My new glasses were slightly oversize and had the irritating habit of slipping down my nose. The curious fact was that no matter how much I concentrated, I was never able to catch them in the act of slipping — and I tried in vain to do this for most of the afternoon. The preferred position was clearly at the bottom of my nose; maintaining them at the top required a constant input of energy, and the probability of the glasses being on the bridge was zero. This was clearly a macroscopic quantum effect that I didn't recall being explained at university. Einstein certainly left a lot of unfinished business.

Pete had finished all the water. His awe-inspiring ability to guzzle liquids was a legacy of years of training at Lincoln University, where the major cultural event was the 'Chunder Mile'. Part of the annual capping ceremonies, the rules required competitors to down a pint of beer, eat a cold meat pie, run 440 yards, and then repeat this ritual three times. The prize was a keg of beer. Some athletes achieved everlasting fame and safe seats in parliament with virtuoso performances such as running in gumboots and using the same footwear to drink from.

Eventually we reached San Juan de Ortega, so named after a person who, as a young man, had befriended Santo Domingo and thereafter devoted himself to building many of the bridges and churches along the Camino. Most of these are still standing today, which was more than could be said for us. We were stuffed, and collapsed on bunks along with about twenty other corpses. It was a morgue, not a sanctuary.

It was not until some indeterminate time later that we could find enough energy to stagger to the showers. I turned the taps on full. One slow, very painful step forward, and: 'Jesus, Mary and Joseph!'

The sub-zero temperature of the water seemed to defy physics. Everywhere else in the world, water froze at 0°C. What sort of country was this where neither classical nor quantum mechanical laws of physics seemed to work? Perhaps the velocity of light in Spain was only 10 km/h.

As penance for past crimes, I forced myself to shower. My feet ached while the rest of me turned blue about as rapidly as litmus paper immersed in a strong solution of caustic soda. I couldn't take any more. Neither could Pete, and as two rosy-cheeked, shambling blocks of ice, we were drawn as if by hypnosis towards the nearest bar. There it took four Coca-Colas with red wine chasers before we could speak.

We settled back to enjoy a bullfight on TV. Because of interference from the surrounding hills, the reception was terrible. Pete asked another pilgrim, 'Do you enjoy bullfights?'

'No. I, ah, don't ah, like much the blood.'

'Then you're in luck, this one is in black and white.'

Later, with some other pilgrims, we tried our hand at sampling local wines from a *bota* in a *bodega*, a large wine cellar. In appearance a *bota* resembles a curved leather hot-water bottle. Traditionally made of pig-skin, it is held at arm's length and squeezed to project a narrow jet of wine into the mouth. Its glass cousin, the *porrón*, has a narrow, tapered

spout out to one side and is used to achieve much the same effect. Success with either model depends on previous training and how much wine has already been consumed. For promoting conviviality, the *bota* and *porrón* are without peer, and almost immediately a wonderful atmosphere of ca-maraderie enveloped the *bodega*.

Adrián was from Guate-mala, spoke flawless English, and was delighted to meet someone from New Zealand. Twenty years previously, while working as a journalist in London, he had been on the verge of emigrating to New Zealand but had eventually decided to return home. It had been his brother-in-law, Alejandro, who had recommended the restaurant in Logroño.

The evening meal was a shared one. The priest said grace and then passed around a large cauldron of steaming garlic soup upon which floated slices of bread. Everyone had contributed something, however modest, and the result was a celebration of the miracle of the 'loaves and the fishes' together with unlimited wine. Initiated by the generos-ity of the parish priest, this had been our first real opportunity to com-mune with fellow pilgrims. Things were definitely looking up.

Later, we found ourselves in a 400-year-old bar, where we tasted a rough, colourless liqueur called *aguardiente* or *orujo*, comprising, accord-ing to our, by now less than reliable informants, 70 per cent alcohol. A few more of those and my feet might have made a full recovery.

It was time to kip down, but en route was the bar where we had earlier watched the bullfight on TV. We hobbled in to be initiated with the Iberian equivalent of a breakfast cereal — the flaming coffee and brandy concoction described earlier. Then, having exhausted the night-life in San Juan de Ortega — two bars and a *bodega* — and desperately trying to maintain some outward appearance of sobriety, we weaved our way to bed.

∫opa de Ajo
Garlic Soup

La sopa is a colloquial term in Spain for the evening meal. Here are a couple of versions of this very simple dish, which around the Mediterranean is considered to be very good for the liver, blood circulation, muscle tone and spiritual health — an easy substitute for a pilgrimage. In the Middle Ages, bread was sometimes only baked once a week and in large loaves so that it lasted longer; since it was often eaten with soup as suggested here, it didn't really matter if it was stale.

Ingredients:

2 green peppers	pinch of saffron
1½ litres water	100 g stale bread
4 cloves garlic	3 Tblsp olive oil
2 ripe tomatoes	salt

1. *Remove the pips from the peppers, and slice. Add to the water along with the peeled cloves of garlic, peeled tomatoes, and saffron.*
2. *Bring to the boil, simmer gently for 5 minutes, and then add sliced bread and oil. Salt to taste.*
3. *Boil gently until the bread swells and begins to break into small pieces. Serve hot from the same pot. Alternatively, soak slices of bread liberally in olive oil, and pour over the bouillon.*

Variation: *In Barcelona, restaurants will often serve this dish with eggs floating in it. For this variation, break an egg into each soup bowl and then pour the hot, cooked soup over the raw egg. Serve immediately. (We cook this version when recovering from a bout of flu.)*

$\mathscr{T}$o Burgos and Back

June 17

$\mathscr{W}$oken at 6 a.m. from a very vivid dream to the sound of a Gregorian chant, it took some moments to collect my wits: one moment I was arguing with the All Black coach about which position I would play and then I found myself in heaven. Playing rugby for New Zealand's national team or going to heaven both seemed rather improbable, but it turned out the music at least was real — well almost — it was a recording, but the sound rising to the upstairs balcony that surrounded the courtyard had the effect of transporting one back to a time when such tunes were 'top of the pops'. I wondered if there would be a short mass, as we hadn't taken communion since leaving Jaca, but the order of the morning turned out to be a large cup of *café con leche*, biscuits, and an early start for the day's march.

It was a shame to leave. I'd often wondered at the number of bars per head of population in Spain and had once considered doing a survey in Zaragoza — a hopeless task, one would be drunk after two streets. The distance between bars in that city was determined by the time that an elegantly clad woman could totter comfortably on high heels in mid summer. Another way to look at this problem was to consider limiting cases, such as San Juan de Ortega. With only six permanent families, and a total of two bars and one *bodega*, which served as a third, this made one for each two families. Then since one family was needed to run each bar, there was actually one per family!

I had scarcely time to take in these amazing statistics when we caught up with Adrián, his sister-in-law, Hema, and wife Valvenera, so named after the Virgin of the Rioja. They were resting by a fountain. Hema's husband, Alejandro, was nowhere to be seen. Except for Adrián, all came from the Rioja. We walked together for the rest of the day at a leisurely pace. Hema and Valvanera talked constantly, and on the rare occasions they ran out of things to say, they sang. They were composing a song about the pilgrimage.

Adrián, Pete and I chatted together about the meaning of life in New Zealand and Guatemala. The conversation turned to the importance of children.

'Always take the time to talk with them. Take my daughter, for example, she loves to talk. You can see,' said Adrián, lowering his voice and indicating to his wife ahead chatting continuously with Hema, 'that it is in her blood. However, even if the subject doesn't interest me, she has honoured me by taking me into her confidence about something that is important to her. So whatever your work obligations, their needs — comfort, sporting interests, school problems, love affairs, etc. — come first. I always talk with children wherever I go. They sense that I love them and they always respond. It helps keep me young.'

In principle, he was quite right. In practice, trying to communicate with emotional black holes such as teenage children could easily make one prematurely old.

We covered several kilometres while I mused further on the subject of my own children. My daughter, Sarah, spent several years locked in her room spitting venom. She is gorgeous now, but nearly didn't make it, as she came perilously close to being strangled for the common good. And as for my 13-year-old son, in a few hours he would be getting ready to play rugby. For these traditional father and son occasions, I usually dressed up in the same old oilskin raincoat that my father had once worn when accompanying me as a child. Then with Sean and some of his mates, we would drive off to some windswept paddock somewhere in the back of beyond. After 40 minutes of mayhem and drama, which usually left the parents exhausted and overdosed on adrenalin, the game would be followed by semi-official and often completely incoherent speeches in Maori or English by the two embarrassed captains, and then by a mad rush for the cakes. A few cold sausages and some dregs of tomato sauce usually remained for the parents, along with a lukewarm cup of tea. Food of champions? This is how traditions are created.

Adrián was also interested in San Juan de Ortega. It seemed that after San Juan was buried in his sanctuary in 1162, many miracles were attributed to him, notably the curing of sterility in barren women, and dumbness in an Irish child.

San Juan was only 17 when he met Santo Domingo, who was then in his seventies.

'It is curious that someone as old as Santo Domingo should have had so much influence over this young man.'

It would be very unusual today for anyone to overcome such a marked difference in age, although the generation gap seemed less marked in Spain, with people of all ages seemingly able to enjoy each other's company.

At the outskirts of Burgos, the temperature was 37 °C. Factories were shut, guarded by furious, salivating dogs, and the streets, strangely deserted.

'Only another three kilometres' was the standard response to directions for the auberge.

Eight kilometres later we spied Alejandro and two other pilgrims drinking in a bar.

'Only another three kilometres to go.'

Approaching the centre of the city, the streets became more and more animated — so much so that it was only with great difficulty that we could follow our friends. We crossed a bridge carried along by the momentum of the throng, jostled by holiday-makers all gravitating towards the epicentre of festivities. Africans in vivid costumes hawking costume jewellery, leather crafts, and brightly coloured rugs from side stalls contributed additional spice to the celebrations, as did their exotic, rhythmic music. In the river, children were swimming, while someone in gaucho costume exercised a horse in the shallows.

The auberge comprised a group of prefabricated huts in the middle of the park — all other accommodation having been exhausted for the fiesta. Surrounding the barracks were thousands of people enjoying themselves Spanish style — eating and singing, drinking and dancing.

We took a quick shower and then a taxi back to a restaurant where Alejandro had arranged for the six of us to enjoy a gastronomic treat at a negotiated bargain price. We had the restaurant to ourselves — everyone else was in the park. Excluding the dessert, everything was prepared from lamb — pâté, sweetbreads, kidneys, lung, intestines and, *la crème de la crème*, a leg of suckling lamb baked in a clay oven. The wine, also by special arrangement, was from the Rioja.

The meal finished with a selection of regional fruit liqueurs which the waiter kindly left on the table. I especially liked a green bitter-tasting one from Galicia. So did Pete and there was little remaining in the bottle by the time we left. This predilection for the fruit of the vine may seen a little foreign to the average Protestant, but I've learnt from experience in France that a little hard liquor at the end of a heavy meal does wonders for your digestion. And the consumption of an entire sheep at a single sitting — well it was not something that could be classified as 'light'. Moreover, as pilgrims we were also in daily need of an anaesthetic for our feet, although to be honest, I was a little confused how each day one tired from the bottom up and then after several medicinal glasses of red wine, one recovered from the head down.

Next was the Gothic cathedral, one of the finest in Europe, and its overwhelming architectural and artistic richness so incredible that I quite forgot to observe carefully the Santo Cristo. This representation of the crucifixion covered with human skin is said to be so lifelike and the bleeding wounds have, we would later learn, been so well imitated by the artist, that it is believed that the statue bleeds and sweats.[5] According to the people of Burgos, it performs miracles and they continue to pray to it when in trouble.

After visiting the cathedral, Alex (Alejandro) and I went for a quiet stroll around the town whilst the others returned to the park to rest. It was my understanding that we were going to buy an ice cream. All of a sudden, Alex burst out into the middle of the main thoroughfare and flagged down a truck. It screeched to a halt, throwing several lanes of traffic into instant confusion. Alex hopped in and I followed suit. Oblivious to the mounting rage of the interrupted traffic flow, Alex negotiated with the driver, convincing him to drive us some 100 kilometres or so back to Nájera so he could pick up his car. I assume that the truck had been heading roughly in that direction, but given Alex's powers of persuasion that can't be taken for granted. Just why he would need a car on a walking pilgrimage was a little unclear, but to enquire further would have been bordering on the sacrilegious. All would be revealed in the fullness of time, and I was slowly learning not to be surprised at being surprised. But what about that ice cream?

The next few hours were spent catching up with all the neighbours in his *barrio* in Nájera, and then getting some special dark ham from his kitchen. On the subject of ham, Alex informed me that this was a speciality of Spain. I casually mentioned that I had friends in France who made a somewhat similar product. Not a very clever thing to say especially when Alex had a large carving knife in his hand and felt that his national honour had been impugned. He glowered momentarily while I rapidly changed the subject to something that was sure to put him in a good mood — the glories of the Rioja, and this time I was especially careful not to make uninformed comparisons with the wines of Bordeaux or Burgundy.

We set off back for Burgos in his old Mercedes-Benz by a circumlocutory route which took us first to Azofra. Alex's plan had finally been revealed. It seemed that after reaching Santiago, he and the others would drive down to Portugal and then back to Seville where they had an apartment. His role was to go on ahead each day as fast as possible without carrying a pack and then hitchhike back to bring up the car with its boot stuffed full of the only wine that a civilised man could drink.

After a quick round of the bars, we found Enrique, a vintner friend of Alex, and together visited his *bodega*. Seen from the outside, a *bodega* can often seem rather nondescript, but, as we had already seen in San Juan de Ortega, an unglamorous exterior often hides a treasure trove of wine and possibly barbecue facilities. This time it was a small winery with a press at ground level and large concrete vats one level down that extended back a good 10 or more metres into the side of the hill. The air temperature in this lower level kept itself around 12 to 14°C all year round — perfect for maturation. Low temperatures during fermentation — the fermenting juice itself would get up around 20°C — may be responsible for bringing out those wonderful flavours so characteristic of these wines. Again, I was assured that there were no added chemicals, and presumably this meant that the fermentation was carried out by families of wild yeasts already on the skins.

The village shepherd arrived — due cause for further celebration and discussion as to the progress of last year's vintage. Such conversations would occur with increasing frequency as the wine matured. Interested in wine production, I tried to discuss crop yields with Enrique, but we hit an impasse on a common unit of surface area: in Azofra a local measure was used rather than the hectare or acre. Jean-Pierre and I had recently come across a similar problem when trying to fathom the following proverb in the patois of the Béarn: '*Dap las higues de Patacàu, que s'en mingje ue mesure, que s'en cague u quartau*' for which a direct translation goes: 'For every measure of figs from Patacàu consumed, you shit twice as much.'

With double the return on your investment, this was a prescription for organic farming. According to the *Béarnise-French Dictionary*, one *quartau* equalled two *mesures* and one *mesure* in turn equalled 20 litres at Pau, 23 litres at Orthez, 24 at Aspe and 16 at Morlaàs and Pontacq. All of these towns or villages lie within a radius of 20 kilometres. This variation in units indicates the degree of insularity that existed when rates of information transfer were referenced to the walking speed of a horse. There were similar local scale variations for liquids and one could easily imagine the arithmetic gymnastics needed for travelling buyers of grain and wine, as well as the opportunity for trickery.

Alex seemed reluctant to leave but eventually we cruised back in the general direction of Burgos with the roof of the Mercedes down and singing (humming in my case) *sevillanas* along with a cassette. We arrived back just after midnight — everyone was sound asleep. Feeling somewhat bloated with white wine, I slept *poco y mal*.

$\mathcal{J}$ambon de Lagor
Jeannette's Smoked Ham

With a ham hanging in the pantry you always have meat on hand should someone arrive unexpectedly. It can be sliced thin and served as an entrée or used in any one of many special dishes. It was memories of this particular recipe from Jean-Pierre's aunt that led me to make indiscrete and almost fatal comparisons with the Spanish *jamón serrano*.

Ingredients:

1 leg pork
coarse salt
pepper

1. *First procure a nice leg of pork. If you have just butchered the animal, leave the leg for 24 hours to cool before beginning the preparation.*
2. *Rub all over with large handfuls of coarse rock salt. Rub the salt in vigorously, especially into the joint, so as to extract as much blood as possible. Place the leg, plastered with salt, in a wooden box sitting directly upon a layer of dry twigs. Cover with a cotton cloth and leave for 15 days to cure and drain.*
3. *Take the leg from the box and knead it strongly all over to squeeze out as much of the remaining blood as possible. Salt again and return to the box for a further 15 days.*
4. *Remove the leg from the box once again. At this point there are many different possibilities. Spanish mountain ham — jamón serrano — is wind-dried without the application of heat or smoke. In Lagor, the preference is for smoking and for this one needs one of those huge, old-fashioned kitchen fireplaces of the type which in former times would have been used for the family cooking. The leg is rubbed over with freshly ground pepper and then hung in the chimney. Smoking takes about one month until it is well dried and a little firm. Hang the ham in a dry environment covered in cheesecloth to keep off flies. Wait another two or three months before eating.*

*H*ortanas and Castrojeriz
June 18

*T*oday was to be a very long (40 kilometre) march in which we would 'discover the immensity of the meseta', that high, sunburnt, quasi-desert plain of Castilla. In anticipation of the heat to come, my blisters were already throbbing after a few kilometres.

After last night's rain the path was covered with snails which Alex ecstatically collected for lunch. Breakfast was in a small bar whose make-shift signs nailed to trees we had been passing for an hour or so before-hand. To amuse ourselves while waiting for the food, we organised a snail race on the table. By 12.30 p.m., and after scratching the first leg of the double, we had feasted on eggs, fried salami, French fries, all washed down with beer and a delicious fruity rosé. Adrián paid — they were so generous that we felt a little embarrassed. We would reciprocate later.

We were now up on the meseta proper and it is difficult to improve on the guidebook's description — this was the sort of landscape and heat that scrambled the brains of Don Quixote. Eventually we made our way down past an agricultural graveyard of old implements and carts into Hortanas. Truly Old Castilla — the town seemed to merge with the earth. In the 17th century it had been described as a handful of shepherds' cottages surrounded by a palisade to defend itself against the wolves. The palisade and the wolves have now gone, but nothing else seemed to have changed. Alex was already chatting to the owner of the auberge who was taking full advantage of a government grant to improve it. By his own admission, he was the most important man in the village, and still single — this statement precipitating jokes about him being a ladies' man 'nudge, nudge, wink, wink,' etc., and the stand-ard retorts.

We were invited to eat with Tio (Uncle), as Alex called him. While he and Alex cooked up a meal of snails, lamb flap, and locally-caught freshwater crayfish, the rest of us talked with a troupe of mounted pil-grims — extremely aristocratic looking men and a particularly attrac-tive girl — who had stopped to water their horses at the village fountain. We chatted as Pete and I casually affected intimate knowledge of equine husbandry, not without justification in my case, as I had seen many cowboy movies and even fallen off a horse once. Somehow this didn't come up in the conversation.

Lunch was in a little room, reserved for Tio's special friends, above his *bodega*. Like his home, there was no evidence of a woman's touch. Pete was not enjoying himself — he wasn't at all squeamish but had decided to draw the line at snails. Personally, I preferred them done in garlic and butter after being cleaned out with salt, but this admission of heresy was dismissed by Alex as completely effeminate: 'Hah, it completely destroys the natural flavour of the snail!'

To my mind, the red wine was incredible — rich-coloured, full-bodied and flavourful, but Alex was not impressed: 'Boof! Natural, but unrefined — it is from Toledo.'

It may as well have been made in Hong Kong — or New Zealand.

I did not enjoy the last 8 kilometres to Castrojeriz. Hema and Valvanera, by contrast, were coping famously — talking and singing, and, up to the crest of one hill, we were cajoled into dancing a *jota* from Pamplona, singing together words which convey the glory of drink. In each village we had passed through, Hema and Valvanera would find something to chat about with the small groups of sunbaked old women, sitting, grim-faced in black, outside their homes. They never failed to raise a smile and then wandered on leaving the world a more cheerful place in their wake.

Pete and I did the last part alone as Alex went back for his car. My feet were aching but we put on a brave front for a group of Spanish tourists who were visiting the church (Notre-Dame du Pommier) which houses an adorable statue of the Virgin. We wandered around looking at the art treasures and tombs. An ancient wooden box with a skull and cross-bones painted on the lid lay hidden in an obscure corner. I quietly opened it up, anticipating a 400-year-old cadaver. Instead of fermenting relics and aged skeletons, it contained nothing but washing-up liquid and a few rags.

'*Merde!*'

The day ended with a shared meal — sardines, bread, olives, wine from the Rioja, which had not too mysteriously appeared with Alex, and an excellent sheep's cheese plus *dulce de frutas* — a quince jam paté. Breaking the crust with us was a bearded pilgrim making the journey barefooted and clothed in a heavy brown robe with matching gourd and staff, looking every bit like a Franciscan monk. Such had been the traditional garb of our forebears in the Middle Ages and, given all the trouble that we had had with boots, bare feet didn't sound stupid.

 # Caracoles
Snails

Snails are a special favourite of my children and, although I have not yet cooked them myself, my sources are impeccable. As Pete and I are still alive, despite eating those cooked by Alex after minimal preparation and no purging, I don't think you can go far wrong. Try at your own risk!

Ingredients:

50 snails	2 bay leaves
salt	1 branch thyme
vinegar	pepper and salt
water	
	For the parsley stuffing:
For the court-bouillon:	2 heaped Tblsp dried
3 litres water	breadcrumbs
3 onions	2 heaped Tblsp butter
3 carrots	4 Tblsp chopped parsley
2 cups good dry white wine	3 cloves finely chopped garlic

1. *Place snails in a covered box or bucket with holes in the lid. After two weeks, bring them out and lift off the off-white film that encloses them.*
2. *Leave snails to purge themselves of any impurities for some hours in a mix of warm water and vinegar supplemented with two handfuls of salt. Repeat this procedure several times; the snails are then ready for the next step.*
3. *Mix the ingredients for the court-bouillon and bring to the boil. Pepper liberally and add just a little salt — the snails should by this stage already be quite salty. Cook snails for 2¹/₂ to 3 hours until they can be detached easily from their shell with a fork. Test a few and leave the rest in their shells. Drain, leaving a few dregs in each shell.*
4. *In a large bowl knead together the dried breadcrumbs and butter. Mix in*

the garlic and chopped parsley to form a homogenous paste. There should be enough parsley to colour the paste green. Salt moderately and pepper. Stuff each shell to the brim with this mixture.

5. *Place under a grill and leave for about 10 minutes until the stuffing has swollen slightly and has developed a 'sunburnt' appearance. This can also be done to good effect over a barbecue.*

ℱrómista Fare

June 19

Only 24 guidebook kilometres today. Pete and I got away earlier than the others but walked slowly because of my blisters. This was spiritual masochism: atonement for sin through pain has always had advocates among Christians despite the fact that Christ's death on the cross made further blood sacrifices unnecessary.

The scenery was not as terrible as I had anticipated: immense expanses of wheat just beginning to turn yellow alternated with equally large ploughed, fallow fields. Yields were low and in another month the landscape would be desert-like. The path followed the plateau, descending on occasions down into widely separated valleys and the odd village. We chatted about everything and nothing — families, children, women, friends we had known and girlfriends we had never known — before finally reaching Frómista-del-Camino.

Pancho was sitting outside the Tourist Office. He had been reappearing at odd intervals riding a small woman's bike with a red triangular flag labelled 'Santiago' at the end of a large aerial. Bearded, and always wearing the same clothes — a description that could equally have applied to myself — he rarely talked, which really was unusual for a Spaniard. He indicated that we follow him to the auberge. It was shut so we sat down outside to experience once again the won-

derful release that always came with taking off one's boots. I should have followed Pete's example and thrown mine away, but it was a bit late now — I'd never break in another pair in the time remaining.

The auberge opened, we tossed our gear on the nearest bunks, and did some cursory hand washing in the bath. Something was wrong — I was vaguely aware that my camera was missing. It had become part of my uniform and I had been wearing it in a small pouch attached to a belt threaded through the base of my prehistoric pack. There, the camera was always easily accessible. While my subconscious acknowledged its disappearance, the rest of me was only concerned with putting my feet up. That thoroughly enjoyable state of suspended animation lasted only until Alex arrived: he had only one passion and that was a single-minded determination to enjoy himself. We found a bar (never a difficult task in Spain) and after a few drinks, asked for the bill. Someone else had already paid, discretely adding our bill to his tab before leaving. This is another tradition that has survived from the Middle Ages — one was blessed by helping pilgrims. Someone else to pray for in Santiago.

Another bar and I was getting hungry. Our basic pilgrim fare usually comprised a bowl of soup, grilled chops and French fries, half a litre of wine, and fruit or yogurt to finish off. Alex had higher expectations, and rather than lower himself to our standards, was negotiating a paella at a special price. As usual he was successful, and so, the problem of the evening meal resolved, we left to find the others. Leaving the bar with the customary, '*Adios, hasta luego*' we passed a man who looked askance at Pete and I. He seemed confused by my fluency in *Castillano* — I had bar-talk off pat by this stage. A few minutes later, he re-emerged, calling after us. His name was Eduardo, we discovered, and he had spent two years working with an Italian mining company at Lake Manapouri in the deep south of New Zealand.

'The best fooking coontry in the world. Excused my Eengleesh, but for twelve years I never speak and sometimes I forget how to say.'

Well, to find New Zealanders in Frómista was little short of a miracle and definitely a good excuse for celebration. We were taken to meet some of Eduardo's friends, Josef and his family, who have made and sold cheese for generations in Frómista. More drinks and we were off to see another *bodega*, or was it a bordello? Sometimes I don't speak so well, in fact, I was beginning to think like Eduardo spoke. As is so often the case in Spain, the evening was developing a momentum all of its own. Eduardo opened a tiny door inset into a larger roller garage door, climbed through and then into a car. The vehicle was many times larger than the small door and I was curious to see how he could reverse the car back through it. If only I'd had my camera, this could have been a real scoop. No, he was just searching for the key to the *bodega*.

The *bodega* was wonderful. Again, the ground level was traditionally used for crushing the grapes and also had a large fireplace and grill for preparing family meals. A stone passage led down to a lower level, where the wine was fermented and stored. Josef arrived with his family, Hema, Valvanera and Adrián, laden with cheese and a large leg of New Zealand lamb roasted Spanish-style in olive oil and lots of garlic. The die was cast; we laughed, praised the food and the wine, and our Spanish friends endlessly sang folk songs originating from one end of Spain to the other. On occasions, Pete also felt the urge to burst into song. I had to restrain him: the only two tunes he could remember were both equally morose — his old school hymn and New Zealand's national anthem. Fortunately Pete got side-tracked by Eduardo.

'I tell you dis. Freendsheep is the only important zing in zee vorld. You write me.'

'I promise.'

Cordero Asado
Roast Lamb

This basic recipe comes closest to our meal in Frómista. While very simple, it is sufficiently different from classical Australasian fare to warrant a try. Give it a go!

Ingredients:

1 leg lamb (about 1¹/₂ kg)	4 Tblsp olive oil
3 cloves garlic	1 cup dry white wine
cracked pepper	3 Tblsp vinegar
salt	

1. *Slice one of the cloves of garlic in half and rub vigorously into the outside of the meat. Then cut small slits into the meat and insert slivers of garlic. Sprinkle the meat with salt and cracked pepper.*
2. *Put the leg in a large roasting pan with the oil and place in the middle of a hot preheated oven (220°C). Leave for 15 minutes, turning the meat once.*
3. *Lower oven temperature to around 180°C and leave for a further 45 minutes.*
4. *Pour the wine over the meat and continue cooking for another 30 minutes.*
5. *Sprinkle vinegar over the meat and cook for a further 15 minutes.*
6. *Remove lamb from the oven and allow to rest for 5 minutes before carving.*
7. *Place the meat on a warm platter and serve with the juices from the pan, and chipped potatoes deep fried in olive oil.*

*M*eson los Templarios and Carrión de los Condes
June 20

*M*y camera was definitely gone. Not wanting to create a fuss, I made the excuse to Adrián of delaying our departure until after the post office had opened. We would try to catch up with them later in the day. Reporting the loss of the camera to La Guardia Civil, I said nothing about my suspicions of Pancho. It had to be him.

'Bastard, why hadn't he stolen my boots?'

We also took the opportunity to send off the tent, and as many other things as we could do without, to the post office in Santiago. There they could await our arrival. Since we were now staying in hostels most nights, there was little point in each carting an extra 5 kilograms just for the fun of it. With the weather so balmy, sleeping under the stars would pose no unpleasantness should the occasion arise.

The walking was uneventful and mostly on tarseal which has covered over much of the original pilgrim route. There was little traffic, the landscape was uninspiring, and the sky dark and ominous. We had been lucky with the weather — it could not last forever.

We entered through the doors of the enormous church of the Templars, Santa María la Blanca, just as the storm broke. The size of the cathedral seemed quite out of proportion to the little hamlet of Villalcazar de Sirga. Originally fortified, it has wells inside to enable the congregation to withstand both sieges and very long sermons. In the 13th century, a miraculous Virgin worked so many extraordinary cures here that her shrine became for a time a rival to Santiago. Amongst the fourteen miracles attributed to her was that of a pilgrim from Toulouse who had vowed to carry an iron staff weighing 56 kilograms, and to lay this at the tomb of Saint James. After praying here to the Holy Virgin, the staff disintegrated into wee pieces, marking the end of his penitence and the forgiveness of his sins.

The church houses the tombs of one Don Felipe and his wife, Princess Christina. Don Felipe had taken holy orders, becoming Archbishop of Seville after its recapture from the Moors in 1248. His brother, the king of Castilla, Alfonso the Wise, had brought Christina from Norway to marry, as his current wife was barren. At the last moment, Alfonso the Indecisive changed his mind, leaving Christina the Dejected. Felipe the Chivalrous, incensed at this callous treatment, abandoned the church, and, in the spirit of self-sacrifice, presented himself as Christina's cham-

pion, marrying his brother's cast-off.

Christina never recovered and died soon after of a broken heart, her tomb becoming a pilgrimage for lovers.

After viewing the remarkable tombs, we rested on the steps of the church, waiting for the rain to stop. We were reminded of another miracle that occurred here when a blind French pilgrim regained her sight whilst similarly sheltering from the rain. The rain stopped after a few minutes. This was always happening. Curious really. I wondered if I should buy a raincoat, but was dissuaded by Pete that this would be an act of some considerable impiety: 'Just trust in the Lord.' That was a spiritual argument which appealed to that portion of my Scottish ancestry as good economics.

As we began the walk out of town, we were waved down by a very old man, dressed in the habit of a medieval pilgrim, complete with a staff with which to fight off wolves and bandits, and a black sombrero, with its characteristic wide brim turned up at the front. This fetching outfit was set off by a large chain around his neck supporting a silver scallop shell embellished with a gold cross. Once proof that a pilgrim had reached the shores of Galicia, the scallop shell became a symbol for the pilgrimmage to Compostela. In French, its name — *Coquille Saint Jacques* — still pays homage to this medieval tradition. So successful was this icon as a marketing tool that successive Popes gave the Archbishop of Compostela the right to excommunicate those who sought to commercialise its sale beyond the environs of the city of the apostle. Unaware of this danger, many modern-day pilgrims proudly display the shell as a badge of honour.

The pilgrim, one Pablo el Mesonero and owner of El Meson Los Templarios, was also acutely aware of the importance of marketing. At staff-point, we were marched into the restaurant where, it seemed, we were expected to partake of the menu. Captured and uncertain of our rights under the Geneva Convention, it was not easy to refuse and clearly presented a much more appealing prospect than walking. And as well we did, for the *menu del día* began with garlic soup, followed by tender, succulent pork cutlets, and then a delicious coconut wafer.

We delayed the restart of our penance by chatting idly with a Dutch pilgrim, who came back each year to explore a different part of the route. Then appeared a real excuse in the form of Alex. Within minutes he was amusing the whole restaurant with his antics. No mean feat, the restaurant was about the same size as a large New Zealand woolshed. Alex knew all about the camera — how? I don't know because I had only mentioned it to Pete and to the police. I told him of my suspicions of Pancho. The conversation returned to food and Alex brought out Red Cross parcels of asparagus and the inevitable Rioja. Pablo joined us and soon Alex had him in peals of laughter. At one stage I thought he had gone too far.

'Do you know how we eat asparagus in the Rioja? No, well watch carefully.'

He placed an asparagus spear about halfway into his mouth. Then taking hold of the tops of both ears with his fingers, he slowly and deliberately turned the ears forward whilst at the same time sucking the remainder of the stalk into his mouth. The result was like a mechanical fairground toy and so unexpected that it sent Pablo into a convulsive coughing fit that saw him staggering red-faced and spluttering to the toilet.

The *coup de grâce* came as we each demonstrated our dexterity with the *porrón*. With some skill it is possible to spray a fine jet of wine onto the side of the nose so that it dribbles down into the corner of the mouth. The really accomplished achieve this with total nonchalance and with no perceptible interruption to the flow of conversation. Pete managed quite well, but my own efforts resulted in the jet hitting the bridge of my nose and the stream of liquid dividing into two parts, both completely missing my mouth. At this point Alex took the *porrón*. With a great sense of theatre, he carefully positioned it at arm's length. A hushed silence reigned as he held everyone's attention for a brief second, and then very, very rapidly, sprayed wine deliberately all over his face. The entire restaurant erupted into laughter and we were immediately the centre of attention of a very large group of ladies from Madrid.

After some negotiation, which had me paying for his meal — live entertainment doesn't come cheap — we slung our packs in the back of Alex's car and walked on. Two hours later his mellifluous voice overtook us. Looking back we saw the Mercedes, the *bota* slung over the driver's side rear vision mirror, and Alex's head out of the window singing one of his favourite *sevillanas*. A quick quench of the thirst and onward again we slogged towards a town with the foreboding name of Carrión de los Condes.

Just outside Carrión, Alex was waiting with our packs. He had arranged for us to stay in a bunk-room attached to the priest's home behind the church, the others having carried on to the next village. According to tradition this church marks the spot where each year up until the Battle of Clavijo, near Nájera, in 845, the Asturians had to pay a tribute of 100 virgins for the harem of the Emir of Cordoba. In this battle, Saint James is said to have appeared, killing 60,000 Moors and routing the remainder. In gratitude, the victors vowed to Santiago that Spain would henceforth contribute each year to the church in Santiago Compostela a bushel of wheat or wine for every acre of ploughed land and vineyard. This tribute was not abolished until 1812 — and to think, as some wag once said, that some people don't believe in miracles!

We threw our packs on the large table, sat down on the bunks, and began our daily foot repair exercises with Pete's knife and vulcanising kit. The other pilgrims were horrified. Amongst them were several old friends from San Juan de Otega. Recently divorced and remarkably cheerful, Jesús-María, for example, had walked from Barcelona dragging all his worldly possessions in a shopping trundler. I never saw him consume anything except a sweet red wine from his *bota*.

Another charming couple, whom we had also met at San Juan de Ortega, insisted on taking us to the doctor. It was a bit embarrassing as the husband was in his seventies and in need of heart surgery. This he refused to have until he had first completed the pilgrimage and presented himself with a suppliant heart before the shrine of Saint James.

Keeping a safe distance from our unshod feet, the doctor laughed, and with only minor differences prescribed much the same treatment as my grandmother would have.

'Get a large bowl, pour in the hottest water you can stand, throw in a packet of salt, followed by your feet. Buy a new pair. No no no! I'm only joking. Sit back, rest, read the paper and enjoy a large brandy and a cigar.'

We followed his instructions to the letter, except for the newspaper. Then we went out to a restaurant recommended by our friends just outside the main entrance to the church and treated ourselves to a meal — vegetable stew, fish, and chilled rice pudding with a slight dusting of cinnamon. Outside, an electrical storm raged and the temperature had dropped about 10 °C. Once again we had escaped.

I turned in early, tried to read a little of the Bible and dropped instantly off to sleep.

*A*rroz con Leche
Rice Pudding

This recipe comes closest to recreating the atmosphere of our meal in Carrión de los Condes. It may, in fact, be even better!

Ingredients:

5 Tblsp short-grain rice	75 g sugar
a few drops of pure lemon essence	1 large knob of butter (about 25 g)
1 litre full-cream milk	2 Tblsp Pernod or malt whisky
1 cinnamon stick	ground cinnamon
1 tsp vanilla essence	

1. *Over a low heat, swirl the rice and lemon essence or juice in the bottom of a saucepan, stirring constantly. Take off the heat and add milk, cinnamon stick, vanilla essence, sugar and butter.*
2. *Bring back almost to the point of boiling, and then lower heat. Leave to just simmer on the lowest possible heat setting, stirring from time to time to ensure that the bottom doesn't catch. Cook for 50 to 60 minutes until the rice become just visible above the surface of the milk. The whole thing should be quite liquid; it will thicken as it cools.*
3. *Remove cinnamon stick and stir in the pernod or whisky. Ladle into 6 individual bowls or ramekins. Sprinkle with cinnamon and then chill.*

☞he Muse of Mansilla
June 21

arned of interminable expanses of wheat, we followed the advice of the guidebook and left early before sunrise. It was so dark that we were lost within minutes, but the ever vigilant Guardia Civil directed us back on the right trail. It was pleasantly warm already. Later it would be unbearably hot. Our feet felt fantastic — a fitting tribute to the curative benefits of cigars, a treatment which has been almost completely ignored by the medical profession.

A road sign indicated that there were cows within 400 m. It was totally superfluous, we had been smelling the animals for several kilometres.

I imagined what I would do to Pancho once I caught up with him. One particularly sweet image had Pancho sitting at the side of the road with his bike wrapped around his head. I pondered on the difficult question of forgiveness.

'Do not take revenge, my friends, but leave room for God's wrath, for it is written: "It is mine to avenge; I will repay" says the Lord.'[6]

The French on the other hand claim that vengeance is a plate to be savoured cold. Perhaps I should just smash Pancho's bike, or head, but not both.

Of Sahagún, we saw little and after a simple meal, decided to continue. At the exit of the town we met our old friend with the coronary condition. He had not been feeling well ever since seeing Pete's feet and had taken a bus to Sahagún. He and his wife had eaten with Alex: 'A superb meal, naturally.'

They all insisted we approach the police about Pancho.

'It is a dreadful thing to happen — he must be Portuguese.'

Reluctantly, I acquiesced to this overwhelming enthusiasm for justice and reported my suspicions. I had little interest — the chances of recovering the camera seemed slim.

It seemed that the police already knew of Pancho — I imagined Alex had spoken with them. They had searched him and found nothing. Neither had he any form listed on the computer. He was from Galicia, hence the strange accent.

I gained the impression that the police knew all of the pilgrims en route to Santiago and, when I thought about it, wherever we had been, even in the most remote and obscure parts of the trail, we often caught sight of the Guardia Civil or their vehicles. Well, we had done our duty, although I was now feeling a little bit uncomfortable about my suspicions. What if it wasn't Pancho? Perhaps I'd just slash his tyres — or his throat!

We walked on without the slightest idea where we were heading. The guidebook description of the route to Mansilla de las Mulas was not reassuring: 'Pilgrim, prepare to suffer; if you are truly to earn your pilgrimage, it is here. Forty kilometres of dead straight, interminable tracks across an immense plain. You will experience a feeling for infinity and for the spherical form of the planet.'

How typically French, they could be poetic about purgatory.

As usual we talked about everything and nothing. I expounded at length upon my theory of the empirical nature of Christianity, explaining how the decision to believe in a God offering unconditional love was essentially illogical. Unless, like Paul on the road to Damascus, one was confronted with the Almighty in a rather spectacular and unequivocal manner, this belief could only be a leap of blind faith. Not that this was without precedent — we, especially scientists, all accept lots of things on faith that defy common sense. In one sense, the aspiring Christian has to be like a mathematician and take on face value a certain number of axioms, in this case the Ten Commandments plus Jesus, and then just see where this leads you. From there on, it is basically an empirical process whereby one attempts to establish a relationship with God and, by His grace, you are increasingly led, often unwillingly, in certain directions. (Actually, just at this moment, I was not at all sure in what direction we were heading, but who cared.) It is this personal relationship with God that usually makes it impossible to convert anyone by logical argument into accepting Christianity. There is a discontinuity seen from either side: on the one hand, there is often rejection of the concept of a deity, and on the other, a personal experience of God totally inexplicable to those who have not had similar experiences: 'And without faith it is impossible to please God, because anyone who comes to Him must believe He exists...'[7]

This tautology presents an almost unsurmountable obstacle, and one which requires the suspension of disbelief. Desperate stuff!

C.S. Lewis makes an argument for the existence of a God as the 'force' behind a set of Moral Laws.[8] These are the ethical equivalents of the laws of physics except for one important caveat. In the case of the Moral Laws, we have the choice whether or not to obey them. Try doing that with gravity! Naturally, most of the time we choose not to. However, we are, equally naturally, outraged when other people make similar choices to our disadvantage, and it is within this moral frame of reference that we formulate our complaints. At this point I noticed that Pete seemed to be sleepwalking through this remarkably clever discourse — Philistine!

We caught up with Adrián, Valvenera and Hema just before reaching El Burgo Ranero. The others were very tired, and Valvenera was favouring her hip. Pete dipped into his bag of assorted medication and found something that he was sure would do the trick. What about a cigar? Whilst we were in Bordeaux, Jean-Pierre had received notice in the mail advertising the skills of one Monsieur Soto, practiced in the esoteric magical arts of the Upper Volta, and promising cures for every imaginable affliction including family problems, sexual incompatibility, impotence, financial disasters, and gambling debts. Between them, Messieurs Soto and Pete would have just about everything covered.

The next refuge was very modern, but had been constructed in a particularly attractive combination of textures — traditional adobe sunbaked bricks of mud and straw with wood panelling. Downstairs were all of the amenities and a large dining room around a huge open fireplace. Upstairs were a further three or four rooms of bunks. Despite these, there was some competition for bedding due to the arrival of a large troupe of cyclists and a similarly large group of Italians. The latter had come replete with wives, children and other miscellaneous entourage, and occupied half the beds in the hostel. Only some of them were walking, with the rest following in a support vehicle. Hema and a large number of cyclists were quite irritated. Pete couldn't have cared less — he reckoned, 'I learnt long ago never to get involved with other people's problems.'

I didn't agree. I've always found other people's problems particularly easy to solve — I'm just continually surprised that no-one ever takes my advice.

After our 60 kilometre stroll we were euphoric and in the mood to celebrate. As usual, in Alex we found a ready companion. He was similarly unperturbed by the rising passions. So, leaving the others to resolve the problem of how to fit 30 people into 16 bunks, we enjoyed a meal of steak and chips, fresh oranges for dessert, and to finish off, a few cautious sips of Alex's *aguadiente*.

Meanwhile, back at the refuge it had been decided that because of the children, and rather than create an international incident in a Jubilee year (a year when the Saint's day falls on a Sunday), the cyclists would sleep on the floor. Walkers, it seemed, had first priority and so we were assured of a bed. Brilliant! Meanwhile the Italians slept on, blissfully unaware of their precarious hold on the bunks.

*N*aranjas al Estilo de Kerikeri

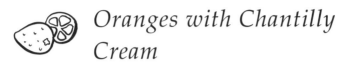

Oranges with Chantilly Cream

Fresh oranges are OK, but sometimes a little post-harvest treatment is warranted. This gem hails from New Zealand, where oranges are a fairly recent 'invention'. In Spain, the earliest references to the citrus family date from the 7th century, and according to Maguelonne Toussaint-Samat, it is even possible that the word in Spanish for oranges (*naranjas*) evokes memories of the original sin, or at least the sin of gluttony.[9] It is said that in ancient times an elephant came across what was then an unknown fruit in the Malay peninsula. The animal (it is not clear what sex) overindulged to the point of exploding. Many centuries later, when humans were still brand new, a man stumbled upon a splendid grove of oranges in the jungle growing from the fossilised remains of the elephant's stomach.

'Naga ranga,' he exclaimed, which, in the Sanskrit of the time, apparently meant 'fatal indigestion for an elephant'.

Ingredients:

10 oranges	***For the Chantilly Cream:***
150 g sugar	**300 ml whipped cream**
6 Tblsp water	**1 Tblsp sugar**
a generous dash of lemon juice	**a dash of vanilla essence**

1. *Peel oranges, slice and carefully remove the bitter white part from the center. Arrange in a bowl.*
2. *In a saucepan, bring sugar, water and lemon to the boil, stirring until it begins to turn golden brown. Now for the tricky part! Place the pan with the caramel in the sink and, holding your face well away, very carefully*

and slowly add 150 ml of boiling water. Stir with a long-handled wooden spoon while it spits and splutters.

3. Pour the contents of the pan over the oranges. Place in refrigerator for at least two hours and serve chilled with Chantilly cream.

4. For the Chantilly cream: beat together all the ingredients, and chill.

*J*ust Desserts
June 22

*W*e awoke very early to the sound of one of the Italians telling his children in a very loud voice, '*Silencio!*'

Our abrupt awakening was followed by a slow start, then by an even longer *café con leche* and *magdalenas* in an adjacent bar. The Spanish support neither silence nor solitude, and the noise in these bars is often overpowering. There are always several different competing conversations, each animated to the point where the participants often appear to be on the verge of violence. These verbal competitions are modulated by noise from several video games and one-arm bandits, not to mention the ubiquitous TV. When someone wants to actually hear something on the TV, the volume control is just elevated, an act which just as automatically amplifies the level of each conversation.

In Zaragoza, José had told me that surveys put Spain ahead of Japan and Italy as one of the noisiest countries in the world. Some years earlier some friends and I stopped at a small village bar in the South of Aragon near Teruel. The bar was almost empty; the silence deafening!

Nothing moved except a barman nonchalantly wiping a few glasses; even the flies were apathetic. We ordered beers and ham and sat down, a little perturbed at such unaccustomed tranquillity.

'This is unnatural,' whispered Yves. 'Perhaps we've mistaken the route and crossed into Portugal.'

At this point entered the village plumber; he headed resolutely towards the toilet, ripped the sink from the wall, and carried it centre stage where he proceeded to belt it with a heavy hammer. The spell broken, an old man staggered from his seat and began to play a video game; life returned to normal.

It was only 20 kilometres to Mansilla de las Mulas, but our collective pace was so slow that it was exhausting. It is much easier to walk at one's natural rhythm than to slow down or speed up to someone else's. The landscape was at least as featureless as the guidebook had suggested — we seemed to be getting nowhere. I was reminded of a propaganda film taken during the German invasion of Russia in World War II, with German officers standing in a similarly featureless expanse of unremitting wheat. The officers kept turning in circles, trying desperately to situate themselves in a landscape completely devoid of topography.

We arrived a little after Alex and before the others. In his usual inimitable style, Alex had been actively studying the form of various restaurants featuring typical cuisine of the region. This technique included chatting up the waitresses, getting invited into the kitchen, and sitting at the right-hand side of the cook. Nothing was left to chance. Such enterprise was not wasted, and come lunchtime, we were welcomed like long-lost relatives. The meal was splendid, owing as much to Alex's public relations skills as to the ability of the cook. We sampled a mixture of local dishes — corned mutton, cod and some other fish that was extraordinarily moist, sweetbreads and tripe in individual sauces, and several bottles of rosé from León. For dessert I preferred *flan* (crème au caramel) while the others ordered a large whisky tart. The latter is a

Spanish favourite in which the whisky seems very much left to the imagination. Not this time, however, as Alex poured a cup of *aguadiente* over it and set it alight, improving the taste significantly.

We strolled back via a couple of bars and a shop selling very sexy gold sandals that would have nicely flattered the ends of my wife's wonderful legs. Funny that I should be thinking of her legs now rather than my own feet. As phantasmagoric images of Delphine's remarkable form drifted slowly in and out of focus in my subconscious, I nearly walked into a wall. Pete had been telling me something in a quite animated fashion and I hadn't heard a word. That would repay him for sleepwalking through my theological perambulations yesterday.

At the auberge we carefully negotiated our way up stairs deformed with age, and took a siesta. Later in the evening, Pete, Adrián and I explored the town which still retains in part the former Roman walls that had once surrounded the entire town. It was very relaxing — the first time in quite a while that we had had the energy to explore, and we were enchanted by the village squares surrounded by arcades. These arcades were formed from the upper stories of wooden buildings supported out over the footpath by ancient buckled columns. A dark, narrow alley led underneath houses built into the upper ramparts to a small entrance in the external wall. From here a dirt path headed down to the river. Looking back from the exterior we could view walls and ramparts as they would once have appeared to pilgrims and soldiers in the Middle Ages.

Flan
Crème au Caramel

Caramel yet again, but why not! In bygone times, crème au caramel was especially popular in wine regions after the harvest, when egg whites were used to clarify the wine. It is still probably the most well-known dessert in Spain.

Ingredients:

For the Caramel:
100 g sugar
1 Tblsp water

For the Cream:
500 ml milk

1 vanilla pod
100 g sugar
zest of 1 lemon
3 whole eggs
2 egg yolks

1. *Pour the sugar with the water in a pot and heat carefully to the point of caramelisation.*
2. *Cool the four ramekin moulds under the cold tap for a few seconds, dry and then pour in the caramelised syrup. Tilt the moulds to spread the caramel evenly over the sides and base.*
3. *Bring the milk to the boil with the vanilla, sugar and lemon zest. Remove from the heat and leave for about 5 minutes to cool and absorb the flavour. Strain.*
4. *Beat the whole eggs and egg yolks in a bowl with a wire whisk.*
5. *Stirring the egg mixture continuously, pour in the boiled milk.*
6. *Pour the cream mixture into the ramekins.*
7. *Place these in an oven tray with boiling water in the bottom to make a bain-marie (water bath). Place in the lower third of a moderate oven. Bake for about 35–45 minutes at 160 °C until a knife inserted in the centre of the custard comes out clean.*
8. *Leave to cool, then chill in the refrigerator overnight. Run a knife around edge, turn out of the moulds onto a chilled plate and serve.*

León

June 23

$\mathcal{A}$fter coffee in a wayside café, Pete and I began discussing diesel engines, for which Pete was an enthusiast. Even petrol-combustion engines were and remain a complete mystery to me. This time I can't foist my ignorance upon a teacher, but rather my father, who was a mechanic. What teenager wants to listen to his father, especially if he risks learning something as useful as how to repair engines? My children won't even deign to listen to me in spite of my being incapable of teaching them anything useful at all.

I have other friends who, like Pete, are apt to become quite loquacious on the subject of the economy of diesel engines. My only direct experience with diesel came after visiting one of these devotees, and, what is more to the point, following a typically unsuccessful argument with my wife. Frustrated at the injustices of her completely unfounded accusations, I absent-mindedly filled up the petrol tank of our car with diesel. The consequences had not been at all economic. Diesel engines should only be approached with extreme caution; a friend says the same thing about women.

The subject changed back to the uneasy relationship between science and religion.

'This God business, Pete, is sometimes pretty hard for a scientist to come to grips with. We are quite comfortable with the duality of light, considering it when convenient as a "particle" with a finite mass, etc., and then when it suits us, we just change tack and think about it as a "wave". We happily switch from one mental construct to another without so much as blinking an eyelid. However, the idea that Jesus could be both man and God fills us with horror.

'I have heard that there have been mathematicians capable of writing down new theorems without proof and which may not even be provable from existing axioms. I tried this technique several times in exams without much success — none actually — but if it were true then it would be as if these people possessed some privileged perspective of reality, some almost God-given insight. Yet the idea that Jesus could have the same insight into spiritual truths seems a bit over the top.

'And then there is Heisenberg's Uncertainty Principle, which implies that all measurable quantities are subject to unpredictable fluctuations and this indeterminism is in-built at a fundamental level. Some scientists have postulated that this could provide an explanation for the spontaneous creation of the universe from the void, that is, Creation without a Creator. The idea seems to be, more or less, probably rather less than more, that since the Uncertainty Principle does not exclude a quantum mistake, why be surprised at an improbable existence purely on the grounds of its low probability?'

And thus I continued to expound upon this learned and remarkable train of thought, citing many other dubious statistical, metaphysical and ecclesiastical notions of doubtful provenance — and generally indulging in such heretical flights of fancy until Pete's patience was eventually exhausted.

'You scientists expect a rational world where every phenomenon is amenable to the intellect. More importantly, you dismiss the personal experience which many people have of God. Did I ever tell you what happened to us when Prudence, my eldest daughter, was very young?

'It was Christmas Eve; Pru was about three years old and she suffered a bad asthma attack. She'd had them before, but never this severe. We had already taken her to the doctor, who prescribed medication that had done absolutely nothing. It was a terrible night and as it wore on, Pru got worse and worse. I don't know if you have ever seen anyone struggling for breath — something that most of us take for granted and never think about. I can tell you that it scared the shit out of me.

'In the morning her condition had worsened if anything; we were about to take her directly to the hospital, and would have done so, if Tissie's mother hadn't intervened: "I'll ring Bill Subritksy, he might be able to do something." Bill owns a farm out further on the peninsula and, as you know, has a charismatic healing ministry throughout Asia and the Pacific. Bill was only too happy to help. I was a bit reluctant, as you can well understand, given Bill's reputation for fire and brimstone, but then what had we to lose. So it was now Christmas morning, and we bundled Pru into the car and drove out to the farm. The first thing Bill did was to ask me if I believed in God. I replied somewhat hesitantly, "Well yes, of course."

'"I mean, do you really believe?"

'"Well, err, um, yes, we go to church most Sundays. Well, except during the game-fishing season, of course."

'"I am not talking about keeping the pews warm — do you honestly believe that Jesus was, and is, the Son of God?"

'"Yes," I replied, too scared to say anything else.

'Bill then turned his attention back to Pru, laying his hands on her. She let out a scream, and went into an immediate spasm, arching her body back until her head touched the soles of her feet. She had never done that before and has never been able to do it since. Immediately she began to breath normally and has never once again been bothered by asthma. Now for me that was proof-positive — a thousand times more convincing than all your scientific claptrap.'

'But um?' I began eloquently. However, Pete was not to be put off.

'I don't think Heisenberg was the only scientist to suffer from incertitude or incontinence or whatever the problem was. From my observations, if you put any scientist on the spot, then his or her uncertainty will grow in proportion to how hard you press them. They are continually trying to find corners in circles until in the limit they are absolutely incapable of making up their minds about anything — it must be a sort of occupational hazard — the Chronic Uncertainty Syndrome.'

There didn't seem much room for negotiation. This personal experience was a very different kettle of fish from Pascal's risk analysis, which argued that it was safer to believe in a God that didn't exist than not to believe in one that did. Perhaps the mystery was more important than its explanation.

Sometime later we looked back and our companions had disappeared. Adrián and the others had probably been side-tracked by Alex for another snail hunt. We decided to press on at our own pace and to meet up with the others at the hostel. The vastness of the landscape stimulated a comparison with the Pacific and its early exploration by Polynesian navigators. Lacking a reliable method of measuring longitude, many of the much later European explorers had difficulty finding islands discovered earlier, and at least in one case had sailed almost completely across the Pacific without making a landfall.

Since today was mostly a mindless tramp on the main road, accurate navigation was of little concern. We entered León and headed for the cathedral, which presented the largest and most obvious target. We would worry about finding the refuge later. Once inside we were completely unprepared for its beauty and the miraculous expanse of stained glass. The windows were extraordinary, and to sit in front of the wondrously carved wooden choir was to be submerged in a kaleidoscope

of colour. For the first time I began to really appreciate the possibilities offered by the changing architectural styles from Romanesque to Gothic.

Our attempts to find the refuge took us all over the city and included a visit to a monastery, where we had a triangular conversation with the Mother Superior. These trialogues had become so common that we were by this stage fully conversant with the rules of the game. I would begin by asking a question. The answer would be directed to Pete, who, because of his colouring and physique, was naturally assumed to have Spanish as his mother tongue. Pete would look slightly perplexed as if mildly confused by one or two minor details of the explanation. I would then interject with a rough translation to which Pete would respond sagely with a drawn-out, '*Sí, sí.*'

And so the cycle would be repeated several times until we were both completely baffled.

Communication in a foreign tongue is not without difficulties. Once upon a time, overcome by the lusty sensations of a Spanish summer, red wine and spicy food, I had bravely attempted to buy some contraceptives in a small Basque village.

'I'm not doing it,' said my Spanish-speaking wife, referring of course to the proposed purchase. 'I never took sex education at A-level.'

Frustrated by, amongst other things, the deficiencies of the English education system, I decided to brazen it out.

'*Prophylacterios, por favor,*' said I, with a confidence I did not feel.

This linguistic fantasy was countered by a blank wall of incomprehension.

I was not to be put off.

'*Contraceptarios?*'

Silence.

Delphine had by this time completely disowned me and was pretending to be fascinated by the fine print on packets of multi-vitamin tablets. As if they would do anything!

By now my imagination was in full flight.

'*Con-dong-a-rillos?*'

I repeated this multi-syllabic apparition about four times, rendering the intonation more and more bizarre with each successive interpretation. This wondrous example of phonetical Spanish was as successful as my earlier attempts. Perhaps the man spoke only Basque — in the Middle Ages travellers had complained about the incomprehensibility of the Basque language. But how could one say something like *con-dong-a-rillos* in a way that sounded as if it were spelt only with Xs and Zs — Basque being a primitive form of Morse code?

The two female pharmacists retired to the back of the shop where they were less at risk from this raving lunatic, and for a moment I was left man-to-man with the male assistant. In desperation I grabbed at the opportunity and also my genitalia, making a few crude but effective gestures. He began to giggle and replied in English, 'Oh, you mean *condoms*, 100 pesetas for a packet of six.'

'Lord have mercy!'

Returning to our current quest, Pete and I eventually succeeded in finding the hostel via the hiking analogue of what is known in mathematics as the method of successive approximations — bouncing around at random, asking directions, misunderstanding explanations, getting lost, and gradually — ever so slowly — narrowing in on the target. The Spanish tendency to offer advice even if they didn't know where you needed to go provided additional opportunity for confusion. And like so many other travellers before us, we grew to dread the sound of: 'You can't miss it, just carry straight on.'

Did this mean that one kept walking in a straight line regardless of bifurcations in the route, or follow the road regardless of direction? But when it came right down to it, who cared? Usually one tumbled upon something interesting.

From the exterior, the hostel had the appearance of a prison. It transpired that the building had once been an orphanage, and the facilities were great. Pete and I were given a room to ourselves with a choice of five beds — how does one divide a prime number into two? Our Riojan accomplices had already arrived. We showered, carried out some minimal but obligatory hand washing, and then took a three-hour siesta. We were getting pretty expert at siestas and as for laundry, well the 'wash and wear' cycle was becoming replaced by a 'wear, wear, wear — and chuck' philosophy. Personal hygiene was rapidly regressing to a standard which would have been quite acceptable in the Middle Ages.

In the evening, and after tortilla and wine, we set off to enjoy the fiesta. Everywhere there was music. I rang José-Luis in Zaragoza to let him know how we were faring, and his daughter, Txuri, wished me a happy saint's day — San Juan. A succession of squares offered every type of music imaginable from pop to Spanish jazz. Most popular of all, however, was in the Plaza de Domingo where several thousand people of all ages were singing local folk songs. The richness and continued popularity of local music in Spain is extraordinary. In most other Western countries, music, like sport, has become a non-participatory spectacle. I have many times tried to buy books with the music and words to some of the more popular Spanish folk songs before coming to the conclusion that they simply don't exist. The reason is obvious: books are for recording cultures already extinct.

*T*ortilla Española
Spanish Omelette

This is one of the most commonplace Spanish dishes, and it is not difficult to understand its appeal. Usually eaten cold, it is ideal for those 'bring-a-plate' occasions.

Ingredients:

1 sprig rosemary
4 medium-sized potatoes
olive oil
6 eggs
salt and pepper

1. *Chop the rosemary leaves.*
2. *Peel the potatoes and cut into small cubes. Sauté potatoes, rosemary and two or three soupspoons of oil over moderate heat until nicely golden. Season with salt and pepper. (Some recipes call for finely chopped onions, but in my experience they usually catch and burn on the bottom of the pan after the egg mixture is added.)*
3. *Beat the eggs in a bowl, add the potatoes and pour mixture into the frying pan together with a tablespoon of oil. Brown the omelette over a moderate heat for 10 minutes, shaking the pan from time to time so that it does not stick.*
4. *Turn the omelette over with the aid of a plate and cook the other side, adding more oil if necessary. As an alternative to turning, you may place it under a grill to cook it from the top down. Don't overcook — the omelette should be just at the point of solidifying in the centre.*
5. *Can be served hot or cold.*

$\mathcal{A}$ **Diversion**
June 24

$\mathcal{T}$oday was to be a rest day. I had arranged to meet friends from Oviedo, Marta, and her colleague Manuel, both of whom were involved in agricultural research in Asturias. We took tortilla and coffee near the cathedral while Manuel quizzed Pete about different aspects of kiwifruit production in New Zealand. Marta handled the translations leaving my mind free, a status which is always rather dangerous. It was impossible not to be aware of the comings and goings of women dressed in leather shorts and other clothes in which my wife would look absolutely fabulous. These little distractions were becoming increasingly common, and to think that my wife had once said accusingly, 'Oh, it's all right for you, you don't have any hormones.'

Hah! The male body is just a seething cauldron of unnatural chemicals: it is a miracle we function at all!

Given a choice of going to Oviedo or sightseeing in León, we opted for the former. In the Middle Ages, León had been an important pilgrimage destination to venerate relics said to be taken in 614 from Jerusalem, where they had been contained in a wooden 'holy ark' built by followers of the Apostles. Fortunately we didn't know this at the time and thus were not unduly disappointed that the cathedral was being prepared for an art exhibition and not open to the public. In the Middle Ages this ark was attested to contain, as well as many other venerable items of inestimable spiritual value:

A large part of the shroud of our Lord,
Eight thorns from his crown,
Bread from the Last Supper,
A large part of the skin of Saint Barthélemy who was flayed alive,
Milk from the breasts of the Blessed Virgin,
One of the 30 pieces of silver for which Judas betrayed Jesus,
Some of the hair of Mary Magdalene with which she wiped the feet
  of our Lord,
A small part of the rod with which Moses parted the Red Sea,
A fragment of the roast fish and honeycomb on which Jesus feasted when

he appeared to the Apostles after the Resurrection,
One of the earthenware jugs in which Jesus converted water to wine at
  the wedding at Cana.

'And anyone who visits these relics, the very reverent Bishop of the same church of Oviedo will remit a third part of the pain owed for his sins. And as well, he will gain one thousand and forty-four years of indulgences.'[10]

This was an age when to touch a relic was to benefit from the power of the saint. Saints were articulate intercessors between a problematic existence on earth and a vengeful God. It was important to have someone arguing on your behalf, and from this follows much of the popularity of the Virgin Mary. For Protestants, the veneration of saints went out the window with the Reformation, but during the Middle Ages and 'in a world where the sacred was everywhere, a relic was an elementary manifestation, accessible to all, of the presence of God.'[11]

Not only had we missed out on one thousand and forty-four years worth of indulgences but there would not be time to visit the Atlantic coast and indulge ourselves with elegant seafood and try *fabada*, the famous Asturian bean stew.

Asturias is also the region of cider and, although we would not experience the ambience of a cider bar this time, the ritual is well worth describing. A bottle of cider is held in one hand well above the head and a large, wide-brimmed glass as low as possible in the other. Just a few hundred millilitres at a time, the liquid is poured into the angled glass, hitting just inside the lip before splashing into the bottom. Without this effervescence the cider is regarded as tasteless. This is many times more difficult to achieve than use of the *porrón*, but the waiters manage without even looking; however, the floors of the bars are covered with sawdust to cope with the less adroit.

Sitting in the square outside the cathedral with Marta, I was once again struck by the incongruities which occur so often in Spain and which are accepted here as quite natural. I remember once outside Valencia seeing a Renaissance Palace sited right next to a car wrecker. Nowhere else but Spain would planning approval be granted for a palace to be built next to a wrecker's yard!

Here in Oviedo, in this old square, heavy-metal 'music' and a 'noisically' equivalent cacophony from several competing video games drowned any opportunity for conversation. Across the square hobbled a very elderly, stooped widow dressed in black, weighed down with memories that would surely have pre-dated the Civil War. From the other direction, platform-shoe-clad teenagers — all bounce and boobs

— tripped clumsily in low-cut tops and jeans across the cobblestones.

A visit to a pre-Romanesque church and hunting lodge brought back memories of an earlier trip to Asturias when I had been invited by Marta and Manual to give a seminar on irrigation scheduling to the region's kiwifruit growers. Here, as in New Zealand, horticulture was viewed as a possible solution to the region's burgeoning unemployment problems, especially as the government was in the process of closing down the coal mines. The seminar had been organised with the help of the local town council in Pravia to coincide with the town fiesta. In cele-bration of this occasion, we were invited beforehand to a special meal with the town dignitaries. Half-way through the third round of peach brandies I realised that the seminar was supposed to have already started.

'Oh, just relax, nothing here ever begins on time,' said the girl sitting next to me, who was to handle the translation, 'and if you get stuck, don't worry, I'm perfectly capable of covering for you.'

And so she was. Trained as a botanist, she spent northern hemisphere winters working in Brazil on field projects in the Amazon, and summers doing simultaneous translations at film festivals in Asturias. She enjoyed the translation work, except for German films during which audiences were apt to get restless; German, like Latin, being incomprehensible until the eventual appearance of a verb at the end of very long sentences. A friend, who had enjoyed a sabbatical year at a German university, tells of a visitor being very surprised at the sight of the attentive faces of students during an exceptionally long and boring lecture. This was such a marked contrast to the normal behaviour of students in other countries, for whom staying awake during lectures is a Herculean task and hardly the highest priority of their university experience.

'Why are they all concentrating so seriously?' she had asked.

'Oh, they are all waiting for the verb,' came the reply.

In due course, my own rendition of a boring seminar had begun, to the clearly audible accompaniment of fireworks and the amplified music of the Rolling Stones: 'I can't get no — satisfaction.'

I hoped the audience wasn't silently expressing similar sentiments. Halfway through the seminar, I had decided to test the translator's promise, and said something absolutely ridiculous. She had just smiled sweetly, and continued speaking as if nothing had happened. The audience nodded sagely. God only knows what she said.

After bidding goodbye to our generous hosts, Pete and I took the bus back over the mountains to León. Back at the auberge, we were confronted with a porter whose dour countenance was the unfortunate result of a lifetime of conscious self-sacrifice combined with sullen disapproval of the comportment of those of more plebeian stock, of whom Pete and I were perfect examples.

'You are not booked in,' he exclaimed in an indignant, and non-negotiating tone.

He made us feel like two drunks who, in search of an after-hours drink, had stumbled upon a temperance meeting. Booking had never been required before and Marta had been assured that there would be no problem with us staying another night.

Pete adopted a fixed look on his face while I contrived to appear plaintive and confused, appealing to the porter's better nature. As this didn't seem to work, I explained, 'We are on a mission from God.'

When that similarly failed to make an impression, I casually mentioned, 'We have been working with the Asturian Ministry of Agriculture on a subject of international importance, and besides, your colleague this morning assured me that there would be no problem with us staying one further night.'

Self-importance achieved nothing, but mention of his colleague brought about an immediate breakthrough.

'Ah, my colleague. Look, what an idiot! Nothing written down in the book. That's the problem. It's impossible to work like this — you can't depend on anyone.'

We didn't understand his problem, but were pleased that he was now happy.

After all that trauma we had a room to ourselves — perhaps they were confusing us with Jesuits. Pete attributed this successful outcome to his 'don't mess with me, buster' look rather than my linguistic abilities. He may have been right but I don't think he really appreciated the delicate and rapid shifts of diplomacy involved.

We could hardly complain at this trivial inconvenience. It had not always been this way. Towards the end of the 15th century, one Jean de Tournai, a tanner by trade, and his travelling companion, sire Guillaume, were astonished at the lack of hostels, by the absence of toilets, and how it was impossible to get warm in the evenings because of Spanish pilgrims hogging the best places close to the fire. In short, he was not happy, but then as the following account indicates, he may have had higher expectations than either Pete or I.

I demanded of my hostess, as was my custom, if she had a good feather bed. I had been dreaming of one all day and was prepared to pay a little extra for the luxury because we had worked so hard, and more especially because of the state of my feet. The hostess mockingly replied: 'We will find you one shortly.' It was late and as there was neither village nor house within two leagues, we had little choice but to stay.

We ate and then went up to our room to be greeted with an evil surprise: beds of straw, threadbare sheets and covers all torn. We lay down and said nothing. Other guests, who had arrived after us, lay down on straw around the fire as was the way of this country.

Around midnight, Guillaume felt the call of nature. There was no chamber pot in the room and so he lifted the cover upon which we were lying, and out of spite for the way we had been treated and the mockery of the hostess, peed in the bed.

Now our hosts who were sleeping in a room directly underneath ours suddenly found themselves submerged in a flood of urine. The patron sprung out of bed, and lit a torch. I could hear everything and when Guillaume realised what had happened, he began to convulse with laughter.

I heard the host coming up the stairs and pinched Guillaume in the bum to stop him laughing. We both pretended to be fast asleep. The light from his flaming straw torch interrogated each part of our faces, but such were our theatrical skills, he had little choice but to tell his wife on returning to his own bedroom that we were sleeping.

About one hour later, when everyone else was again sleeping, I, in the same manner as Guillaume had done earlier, raised the sheet and emptied my bladder. Once again the pee-pee flowed between the floorboards and dribbled onto our hosts. The innkeeper got up once again, lit his torch and mounted the stairs whereupon he found two pilgrims still dead to the world. He grumbled his way back to bed. Two hours later, Guillaume and I opened the front door and fled out into the moonlight to the screams of rage from the innkeeper and our laughter.[12]

'Hey Pete, is there a chamber pot under your bed?'
'No worries, mate, we're on the ground floor.'

⁀Atún al Estilo Japonés
Sashimi

In New Zealand, tuna is mostly canned, or used for bait. In Spain, on the other hand, it forms the basis of many dishes and is a very common tapa. I have explored many Spanish recipes, but when Pete first introduced me to sashimi or raw tuna eaten only few hours after it was caught, I became a whole-hearted enthusiast for this Japanese method. The best way to cook tuna is not to cook it!

Ingredients:

fresh tuna

soy sauce
wasabi

1. *Catch the fish — yellowfin or albacore. It must be fresh and not frozen!*
2. *Cut off slices in towards the centre of the fish. Trim off the skin and cut into portions about 5–10 mm thick depending on the texture. You need to be able to lift it up with chopsticks without the fish falling to pieces. The taste will also vary a bit depending on the thickness.*
3. *Take a piece of fish in your chopsticks, dunk into a bowl of soy sauce mixed with wasabe (Japanese horseradish) to give your tastebuds an extra thrill and to clear the sinuses. Eat immediately.*

*L*eón to Astorga

June 25

I slept badly because of the heat and the noise of the fiesta that continued most of the night. *Café con leche* and *magdalenas* put me in a better frame of mind; a wonderful breakfast after which one can walk 30 kilometres without effort. I have absolutely no confidence in that Swiss fetish for beginning the day with a plate of hydroscopic cereals floating in a bowl of milk and a garnishing of sun-dried pine cones and raw rocks. My wife is addicted to this form of self-abuse, but after some initial experiments I found that it was just incompatible with cycling to work — in fact, it was potentially very embarrassing; culinary masochism is at least as indigestible as its spiritual equivalent.

The route was boring and my right shin was beginning to get quite painful. It had been aching since we arrived in León and I had hoped that a day's rest would have cured it. Typical — one blister-free day of bliss and then something else packs up. After several kilometres and over a cup of coffee, I mentioned it to Pete who replied with the rather serious expression of one trained in things biochemical and metaphysical, 'Shin splints, got them once training for a marathon, bloody painful!'

'So I've noticed — will it get better by itself?'

'Hmm, might take a while but I've got some anti-inflammatories somewhere,' he replied, groping around in his pack. 'Threw out most of the containers to save weight and put all the pills in this one bottle. Here, I'm certain this is the one.'

He held up an innocent-enough looking capsule.

'Don't swallow it! According to the pharmacist it is designed to be taken up the anal passage. There it is quickly absorbed into the bloodstream and it should be much more effective. Quite interesting really.'

'Interesting?'

I looked in horror; it was a family tradition to be suspicious of suppositories. My son's reaction, when confronted with the possibility of our returning to France for 12 months, had been characteristically succinct. He had lived there previously as a four-year-old. Seven years later, his most vivid recollection of life in Provence was: 'Doctors there stick things up your bum! I don't want to go!'

However, it was also true that the children used to recover very quickly — whether because of the indignity, or the efficacy, of the treatment, I was never too sure. I decided that with seven children, Pete's knowledge of illness should be encyclopaedic, and so retired rather dolefully to the toilet to insert this capsule discretely into the appropriate orifice. I walked very cautiously back to the table, cheeks tightly clenched. In biblical times, the stricken would exhaust themselves in prayer, only throwing themselves upon the whims of modern medicine as a last resort. Had I explored all the options?

'Well, is anything happening?' asked the apothecary's apprentice.

What did he know that I didn't?

The festering fuse went off about an hour later, sending shock waves through the rectum. The next part of the day was an unmitigated disaster. Pete's panacea did nothing whatsoever for my shin, but cured me of constipation more effectively than two tonne of raw cereals.

I had little time to dwell on the relative efficiency of modern-day suppositories in terms of tonnes-equivalent of figs: the next several hours were spent hopping painfully at high speed and, like a diarrhoeic dog, systematically marking the occasional low shrubs which offered the only privacy from oncoming traffic. Oh for a long-drop — I would have dived straight in! It wasn't just our laundry habits which were adopting medieval proportions.

Lunch provided an opportunity to wrap the shin in ice. With the benefit of hindsight, it now seems that the problem wasn't only shin splints, but also an infection; this had clearly not been confined to the lower leg, and had already provoked a severe case of dementia. To prove this, I readily agreed with Pete's suggestion to carry on to Astorga. Why? I'm not sure, we had already walked 40 kilometres.

We crossed the celebrated 20-arch Romanesque bridge over the Orbigo, once the route of a retreating British army in the Napoleonic Wars, and earlier still, the scene of a famous chivalric jousting match. Here in 1434, another Jacobin Holy Year, a Leónese knight — Don Suero de Quiñones — and nine companions in arms, challenged, in honour of his lady, any European knight who wanted to cross the river. The tournament lasted 30 days, 300 lances were broken and there was one death. Wimps! Jousting was clearly less dangerous than rugby. At the end of the tournament, Suero de Quiñones made the journey as a simple pilgrim to Santiago de Compostela, depositing there a golden bracelet which is still worn today by the processional bust of Saint James. Cervantes would later use Suero de Quiñones as a model for his Don Quixote.

Beyond the bridge the scenery was again boring — I was also feeling a bit depressed as the pain in my leg increased. My pace got slower and slower the closer we got to Astorga. This was another relativistic effect that Einstein overlooked — distances increase in the afternoon.

Craving something sweet, I stopped at the entrance to Astorga and drank three large glasses of lemonade in quick succession. It wasn't at all clear that I could make the next kilometre to the refuge and it was tempting to remain in the bar listening to three old men arguing over a game of cards.

Pete came back for me after unsuccessfully seeking the refuge. Impatiently I forced myself to walk on, asking directions from each person we passed. It transpired that the usual refuge was closed and we were directed to a special camping ground: rows and rows of large red tents each containing a pile of mattresses. Portable buildings housed toilets and cold showers as well as some first aid facilities. We were allocated a tent with an elderly German couple.

Leaving our bags in the tent we hobbled back to the square to find a telephone so that Pete could ring home. With conspicuous difficulty we explained to the barman that Pete wanted to ring New Zealand — we had long since given up being Australians, it took almost as long to explain and we then had to endure everyone hopping around the bar imitating kangaroos. The barman kindly emptied the till of change and Pete stood at the bar surrounded by columns of coins looking like Uncle Scrooge in the children's comics. I don't know how he could stand it — every time I'd tried to ring Delphine, it had been impossible to concentrate on conversation as '*pesetas* remaining' flashed past like a video on fast-forward.

Pete eventually got through — it was the middle of the night in New Zealand, but Tissie was up feeding Eddy, my godson. I relaxed in a chair behind a glass of wine and a plate of *croquetas*, which, although not up to the standard of Blanca's mother's, still filled the small gap that had once been a stomach. Lean and fit, a reformed picture of health; how come I didn't feel so good?

It was early evening and the locals were catching up with friends and family. I think I was beginning to get delirious — everywhere I looked, we were surrounded by absolutely stunning women. Even for Spain this was exceptional.

Back in the tent, the German man turned out to be Dutch and before retirement had been an international authority on the physics of thin layers. Rolf was delighted to be able to speak English: 'Spanish is so guttural, it sounds like Arabic.'

He and his German wife, Christine, were thoroughly enjoying their pilgrimage. They were amateur botanists.

'There are no insects or birds left in Germany now. You should be careful in your country with pesticides — eventually they get into the waterways and your grandchildren will suffer. The hand of God is to be seen in the beauty and intricacies of nature and the laws of physics — not in the silly miracles that the Catholic church would have us believe. We must protect God's creation.'

It is curious how many Christians want an ordinary God, a supernatural being with no balls. If God were the Creator of All, why just limit the Author of the Universe to setting the rules, flicking the first switch, and thereafter sitting back to enjoy the spectacle like an extraterrestrial video game? Amusing, but not very interactive. It may have been an interesting point to debate, but not tonight — we had walked 60 kilometres again! All I wanted to do was fall instantly asleep and wake up with a new leg.

*C*roquetas
Croquettes

This dish takes a bit of practice, but the taste is adorable. It can be made with a béchamel sauce, but this version from Blanca's mother, María-Dolores, gives a thicker mixture.

Ingredients:

For the sauce:	*For the coating:*
¹/₂ cup flour	1 cup flour
1¹/₂ cups milk	2 eggs
2 egg yolks	1 Tblsp oil
salt, pepper and nutmeg	1 tsp water
2 Tblsp butter	salt and pepper
¹/₂ cup chopped grilled bacon	2 cups dry breadcrumbs
¹/₂ cup gruyere cheese	oil for deep frying

1. *To make the sauce, place flour in a heavy saucepan, gradually blending in milk with a wire whip. Stir over moderate heat until mixture begins to clump.*
2. *Remove from heat and blend in the egg yolks. When smooth, beat over heat for 2 minutes to thicken the sauce. Remove from heat, beat in the seasonings and butter.*
3. *When the mixture has slightly cooled, fold in bacon and cheese. Cover and chill for several hours.*
4. *To make the coating, pour the flour into one bowl, beat the egg, oil, water and seasonings together in a second, and place the breadcrumbs in a third. Start a little production line: scoop 1–2 tablespoons of the chilled sauce mixture and dredge with flour. Shape with fingers into small cubes or cylinders and then drop into egg mixture. Coat the entire surface. Drain on a fork and then coat evenly with breadcrumbs.*
5. *Deep fry four or five croquettes at a time in very hot oil, turning carefully until nicely golden all over.*
6. *Can be served hot; but in my opinion, the taste is much better if left over night and eaten cold.*

*M*alaise and Matadors

June 26

I slept badly again — my ankle and shin were too sore to get comfortable. Rolf and Christine rose at 5 a.m., and we left soon after. After a few painful kilometres we came across them resting in the shade. Their philosophy was to go slow and enjoy each part of the journey. There was certainly a temptation to concentrate on how far there was to go rather than just enjoy each moment, a temptation that applies equally to life in general. We joined them and mused on the scenery — the agriculture always seemed more interesting as the topography began to get more broken. The less suitable the terrain for modern machinery, the smaller were the fields, the older the tractors, and the more people, often entire families, to be seen in the fields.

Walking together later, Rolf and I watched Pete and Christine fade into the distance at a speed that I was not sure even Pete could keep up for much longer.

'Your wife, she walks fast.'

'That is true, but not grounds for divorce.'

We talked about the importance that work is given in our consumer society.

'I've enjoyed my work immensely, never discovered anything useful at all, but I had a lot of fun. We are here to enjoy God's works, but the problem is that the young are indoctrinated from birth about the virtues of work, and seduced by television that happiness is commensurate with greater and greater material comfort. By the year 3000 machines will do most of the work and then perhaps people can enjoy God's creation — if anything is left.'

After an hour we stopped again. This time Christine collected some wild herbs, moistened them with water and then bound them tightly against my shin as a poultice.

'I married a witch,' was Rolf's only contribution.

The scenery viewed from the shade of the oaks was the epitome of bucolic bliss. On the gentle slope across from us a cowherd lay on her back, basking in the sun. Wild flowers of all colours abounded, the only sounds were those of birds and cowbells, and the air was perfumed by herbs.

'Ahh, it smells like heaven,' sighed Rolf.

He explained how they participated in a Catholic church in a small town in Germany close to the Czech border. Christine sang in the choir. However, they didn't personally accept the Pope as the mouthpiece of God — the concept of papal infallibility was apparently quite a recent invention. Rolf continued, 'There is too much bureaucracy in the Catholic church, and the Protestants are no better. Dogma, duty and discipline are stressed at the expense of love, freedom and joy. Living museums! It is only in places like this that one can observe the completeness and beauty of God's creation.

'Another thing I don't like about the church is there is no place for modern science. It is seen as a threat. Eventually gravity will make everything condense, the "Big Crunch" will be followed by another "Big Bang" and we'll start all over again.'

He was certainly right about the church; the veracity of the hypothesis of a successively expanding and contracting universe is, as I understand it, still being debated. Science has often been viewed by the church and many Christians as a subversive activity, the furore over evolution and the church's treatment of Galileo being the two best-known examples. The debate over Darwinism has been particularly unfortunate because it set such entrenched viewpoints that even today it is difficult to discuss the issue without being labelled as either a right-wing fundamentalist or a heretic. While ethical and moral questions lie outside its frame of reference, science deals with the mechanics of how the world is, and we have every right to explore the mysteries of the universe. It is just hard going.

At the next rest, Christine bandaged up Rolf's leg as well as my own. He had a similar problem and a doctor had suggested he rest for three days. Rolf was keen that I accompany him on the next part of the journey by train, but I had no intention of giving up, even for a few days. If it is true, as some people contend, that I have enjoyed a career in science despite being dim-witted, why should one leg be a handicap for a pilgrimage?

I lay back on my pack and closed my eyes. The next thing I knew I was being woken by the sound of my own snoring. I opened my eyes to Pete's laughter as he no doubt remembered my earlier complaints about his snoring in the tent. It was curious how I couldn't sleep at night on a comfortable mattress, yet lying here on the ground, I was able to snooze like a professional.

At the next village we took coffee and a snack of ham — *jamón negro*. The barman also gave us, as a gift of the house, a plate of anchovies pickled in vinegar and garlic. I was never sure whether these repeated acts of kindness were due to the privileged status of pilgrims or just another reflection of the generosity of Spaniards.

I conquered my pride and bought a walking stick. Rolf and Christine only intended to walk 20 kilometres today, and against their advice we carried on. Ahead lay the Mountains of León which marked the end of the 'interminable and dusty plain'. The guidebook spoke of a small, picturesque and tranquil track by which we would cross these minor obstacles, a description somewhat spoiled by references to peaks up to 1500 metres. It was certainly picturesque, and fragrant with the odours of rosemary and thyme intermingled with those of broom, heather in flower, and other shrubs. The 'interminable plain' gave way to an 'interminable range of hills'. I no longer believed distances in the guidebook — a true measure of distance between two points was related to how much effort was involved in walking between them — Spain was definitely not a subset of Euclidean space.

We rested frequently, and although my leg seemed slightly better, I was not sure it would hold out to El Acebo. We stopped in a village for a meal along with lots of cyclists and a band of school children, all on their way to Santiago. I had no appetite and the wine was dreadful — the first bad bottle I'd tasted in Spain. Even diluting it with lemonade didn't improve the taste. This didn't seem to bother Pete.

'It's the same colour as Rioja, what's your problem?'

Pete went on ahead to organise some accommodation while I limped onwards as best I could. Damn leg was beginning to get on my nerves.

The scenery was dramatic, with steep-sided hills and very deep valleys. The peaks were so high there would be snow here for much of the year. Mist, beginning to form in those secluded portions shaded from the evening sun, added to the atmosphere of mystery and isolation. Perched upon a steep ridge deep down on the other side of a valley was a small village. It was difficult to imagine how it could be reached except by helicopter or suicidal donkey.

Two men in a very old car going in the opposite direction stopped and asked if I needed a lift to Molinaseca. As a general rule, it is only people in old cars that ever pick up strangers. Apparently Molinaseca was about 15 kilometres further — about 5 or 6 hours walking in my present condition.

'I'm heading for Acebo.'

'Oh, there is nothing there, nothing at all!'

I stubbornly refused a lift and continued. It was beginning to get dark, I could end up sleeping out tonight. That wouldn't be the end of the world, but rather than make a decision I carried on slowly, making the most of the scenery and the late evening light.

I reconsidered hitchhiking, but all attempts were unsuccessful — a sequence of people in nice cars! I gave up and resigned myself for the long haul. Almost immediately a car stopped in front of me, and a family on their way back from León insisted I get in — I didn't protest. We communicated in a mixture of Spanish, French and English. They were also unhappy about us staying in Acebo — I'm not sure why because on arrival it appeared rather quaint — a small collection of stone houses with slate roofs. Pete emerged from a bar at that moment and after a quick discussion we decided to follow the standard advice and continue to Molinaseca by car — what a marvellous invention is the internal combustion engine!

At Molinaseca, the river had been dammed up for swimming and bordered with a large sandpit to create a beach at one side for the children. Unfortunately, the camping ground was a good couple of kilometres out of town, and although I was hardly in any condition for further walking, the lure of a swim proved irresistible. I only made it to the first bar, where there was a televised bullfight from the fiesta in Burgos. A marvellous spectacle — three courageous matadors and six brave bulls. One matador, who had been treating the bull rather disdainfully in a very successful effort to appear flamboyant, got caught between the shoulder and the horns and was tossed effortlessly up into the air. Miraculously, he landed between, rather than on the horns, avoiding certain death. The support team managed to divert the bull's attention and the fight continued as if nothing had happened.

For most Anglo-Saxons, the corrida is anathema. Me, I love them: the combination of pageantry, colour, ballet, danger and courage is completely intoxicating. I'm seduced from the moment the *alguazil*, dressed in the costume of a 17th century police officer — hat with white feathers, black silk cape and white crimped collar — enters the ring mounted on a prancing horse to receive the keys of the *toril*. Behind him follows

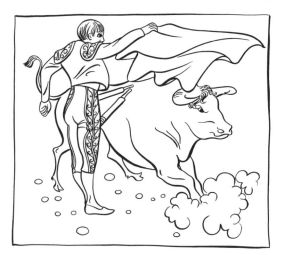

a procession of matadors, banderilleros and picadors.

From the *toril*, the bulls are liberated through a dark corridor from whence 500 kilograms of muscled fury explodes into the ring, eyes partially blinded by the mid-afternoon sun. At this early stage of the contest, the bull is at his most impressive, but least dangerous. As the duel continues, he rapidly learns both the rules and to conserve his remaining strength. In fact, he would become progressively harder and harder to dominate if the fight were to be prolonged. A corrida bears absolutely no resemblance to the game of cricket, and one should not expect to see an equal contest. The result is inevitable, with the high point for the bull coming when he takes on the mounted picador. Thereafter it is all downhill, with the best he can expect being a noble death. Jean-Pierre, an aficionado of the corrida, likens the contest to an interview, where the role of the matador is to bring out, in the most artistic way possible, the best qualities of the bull, its strength, courage and character, a combination termed *la lidia*.

According to an earlier pilgrim, A. Mabille de Poncheville, the origins of the corrida are not hard to find.[13] For a pastoral people, the original reason for a bullfight was to rid themselves of useless and possibly dangerous bulls. And it is...

not a vulgar execution but a contest which puts into relief, the audacity and dexterity of young men, encouraging in them those two qualities, which together contribute to the development of supremely virile and elegant man.

De Poncheville, too, deplored the false sensitivity of his period — the 1920s — when as today those who have never attended a bullfight discredit it a priori as inhumane.

Today's corrida is a stylised version of a Mediterranean tradition which existed in Crete some 18 centuries before Christ. Its character cannot be gauged by reading books: one has to participate in the pageantry, to enter fully into the spirit of the occasion, and to enjoy the crowd and the music. When my children were very young, we went with Txuri (the daughter of José and Blanca) to a bullfight in Huesca, a town in the north of Aragon lying between Zaragoza and Jaca. That day the newspapers reported some remarkable demonstrations of valour in the ring, but what bears recapturing here is the atmosphere in the crowd. Our neighbouring spectators, if somewhat exigent in their expectations of the matador, were nevertheless very welcoming: we were invited to share from the *bota* and lavished with bread rolls and fresh slices of ham carved on the spot. At one point, I glanced round to see the three children trying to light a huge cigar, to the immense amusement of their new friends. Out of concern for their health, I confiscated this dangerous weapon and showed them what to do with it.

Many years later, it is difficult to apportion blame between the heat, the excitement, fatigue or even perhaps to an obscure allergy to alcohol, but what is clear is that, in the fullness of time, the two gentlemen who had assumed the major responsibility for provisioning our section of the multitude, became more and more unsteady on their feet. This unsteadiness, together with a certain slowing of reaction time, had the following consequences. With his back towards the ring, one of these fine fellows was leaning over the ham concentrating as best he could on the delicate task of cutting off a few more slices when the crowd erupted at the sight of a particularly well-executed and dramatic pass in the arena below. Caught unawares by this unexpected turn of events our friend turned, abruptly raising the ham, which his erudite companion, innocently returning from a short visit to the loo, caught under the chin. A haymaking blow; the victim collapsed instantly to the deck, where he tried groggily to recapture his senses, totally ignored by the crowd, who were too preoccupied by the events in the ring, and his friend, who stood vaguely waving the ham above his head. With an immense effort, the innocent tried valiantly to struggle to his feet, and would probably have succeeded, if he had not collected a second heavy blow to the head as his erstwhile colleague, exhausted with the effort of holding up this huge ham, dropped his arm. Out for the count this time, it took almost half a *bota* of wine to bring him, if not fully to his wits, at least to the point where he could distinguish *torro* from matador. The children thought that it was a masterly performance and talked about it for weeks afterwards.

A poll of French students on the question of whether or not the corrida constituted an art form received nearly 70 per cent of positive responses south of the Loire and only 35 per cent in the north.[14] Being from further south than anyone in France, it should be obvious where my sympathies lay.

$\mathcal{T}$raditional English Empanada

I was no mood to appreciate food just at this part of the pilgrimage, but if I had been in better shape then I would probably have looked for an empanada to compare with this steak and kidney pie. This particular dish is a tribute to my father who until his death was engaged in a quest to find the perfect pie crust; the dough mixture comes courtesy of my sister, Janet, with the message that it is idiot-proof.

Ingredients:

For the pastry:
2¹/₂ cups flour
2 tsp baking powder
250 g cold butter
1 cup milk
2 tsp wine vinegar or 4 tsp lemon juice

For the filling:
1¹/₂ medium onions
1 clove garlic
olive oil

500 g braising steak, cut into cubes
200 g kidney, prepared as for 'Kidneys in Sherry' (page 37)
1 Tblsp flour
salt and pepper
2 cups chicken stock
a generous handful of chopped, strong-tasting field mushrooms
a knob of butter
1 egg, beaten or milk

1. *Make the dough in two portions using half the ingredients for each. Sift flour and baking powder into a bowl. Slice the butter finely, and cut into the flour. Run hands under cold water, and then mix in the butter between thumb and fingers until the mixture resembles breadcrumbs. Add milk and vinegar and form the dough, minimising the amount of handling. Leave to rest for an hour in the refrigerator.*
2. *In a heavy frypan, fry the chopped onion and garlic in olive oil until the onions go soft. Remove from pan. Sprinkle the steak and kidney with flour and brown in the same oil used for the onions. Season. Return the*

onions to the pan, pour in the chicken stock and simmer uncovered for 45 minutes.

3. *Meanwhile fry the mushrooms in a separate pan in olive oil and butter. Sprinkle with salt as they brown.*

4. *Add mushrooms to the meat and onion mixture and continue cooking on low heat for another 15 minutes — be careful to ensure that some liquid remains to make a gravy. Sprinkle finely with a little flour to thicken if necessary. Remove the garlic.*

5. *Press both dough mixtures with the heel of your hand to prepare for rolling. Roll out to make two sheets of 5 mm thickness.*

6. *Cover the bottom of a greased, 25 cm diameter pie tin with one of the sheets of dough. Pour in the filling. Place the other sheet on top and stick the edges together by pressing down with a fork. Decorate with leftover bits of dough and brush with beaten egg or milk.*

7. *Prick the top with a fork several times and cook in the oven at 220 °C until golden.*

$\mathcal{M}$olinaseca to Ponferrada
June 27

$\mathcal{I}$ slept well, only vaguely aware of an electrical storm which in the morning Pete described as the most dramatic he had ever witnessed. When I woke up, my torpid body was swathed in a foetid, sweat-drenched sleeping bag, hermetically sealed at the neck. Perhaps I wasn't very well? Pete was convinced of it, after all I had not enjoyed the wine yesterday. The ancients said that there were three forms of misery — sickness, fasting and travel. Afflicted with all three, what chance had I? Anyway, the leg looked a little better and so we decided on an easy day — just the 18 kilometres to Ponferrada.

We started off strongly enough, but were soon out-distanced by a man on a donkey. Closer to Ponferrada was one of the prettiest villages we had yet seen in Spain, with old wooden houses, occasional patio gardens and second-storey balconies graced with climbing plants and garlands of drying corn cobs. Standing in dramatic isolation a little further on was a very modern and obviously more expensive home lacking the charm of the smaller village cottages. As yet another example of Spanish incongruities, this chateau overlooked the municipal dump!

Ponferrada came up fairly quickly and we made our way up a very narrow street to confront the magnificent 13th century castle of the Templars: a fairytale castle from a child's storybook. After a quick look around the exterior we continued on to the tourist office and leaving our packs there, set off to explore the town. Pete claimed that I needed a haircut. He had had his locks shorn in Logroño and had come out looking like one of the Beagle Boys, raving about the barber's skill with the scissors. Against my better judgement I sat down and waited my turn whilst reading in Spanish about the innermost secrets of the Princess of Wales and Rachel Hunter. A young man with a head in the style of a Hare Krishna devotee asked me in French what style I would like. I pointed to Pete and replied, 'Not like his!'

'OK.'

About 20 minutes later and after watching the incessant movement of scissors getting closer and closer to my scalp, I emerged with even less hair than Pete. Never having heard of repetitive strain injury, the barber's dependence on scissors and razors was in total contrast to New Zealand, where barbershop techniques follow methods perfected for sheep shearing.

Next stop, clothes shopping. On the way we met up with two other pilgrims, each quite distinctive in their very different ways.

Both were from Barcelona. One resembled a refugee from Woodstock, with John Lennon glasses and very long hair (just at that moment I was quite conscious of hair length) and was accompanied by a beautiful white Labrador dog. The other, short, dapper and with a handlebar moustache, looked like an English pilot in the Battle of Britain. Both his boots were splitting around the sides.

'My feet were not so wide one month ago.'

They had got caught up in the hills in the electrical storm.

'Fooken rain,' he said several times, savouring every syllable. What a wonderful thing to be able to swear so fluently in another language.

I bought T-shirts, clean underpants, and a pair of shorts. I decided to wear them straight away.

'Would you like that I wrap up your old clothes, sir?'

I looked nostalgically down at the shorts that had protected my manhood for some 500 kilometres and which my wife had been trying unsuccessfully to throw out for five years. The crutch had disintegrated. I held up my ragged underpants to the light — a chaotic collage of holes delineated by miscoloured and stained threads. They were like the universe — mostly nothing. This public display was a mistake: Pete turned green and moved away, while the shop assistant glanced furtively around to observe the effect on his custom — there was none, the shop had been discretely evacuated. Still, it was not easy to overcome the emotional and physical attachment to these rags. But if I couldn't buy Delphine a gold watch, I could at least make a burnt offering of these sacred items. Carefully I hid the underpants in the shorts' pocket

— I didn't want to poison the person who emptied the rubbish.

'Where is your bin?'

The shopkeeper looked as apprehensive as Pete was relieved: 'Praise be to God, I couldn't walk much further with those shorts!'

Huh, since when had he got so sophisticated?

We took a siesta. I didn't sleep but Pete dreamt that I snored for three hours. Where did he get such fanciful ideas? Then it was time for a round of stuffed peppers, and to settle back over a glass of red wine and watch the highlights of bullfights from around the regions. We seemed to be out of phase with the bullfight circuit, but the TV coverage was better than nothing. Pete was enthralled, it was the first time that he had seen it in colour. A banderillero on horseback gave a spectacular display of horsemanship — my father used to tell me how accomplished riders control the horse with their knees. That was probably true, but I had always found that one needed more than just two hands to hold on with.

That night we were to sleep on a mattress in a gymnasium. A nurse withdrew some pus from my heel and filled it up with an antiseptic fluid. It must have been good for me, it stung like hell.

*P*imientos Rellenos al Estilo de Delphine
Stuffed Peppers

Not exactly what Pete and I often ate in bars along the route but rather Delphine's adaptation and one which takes cognisance of the difficulty of getting fresh tuna in Australasia, unless you are like Pete and can catch it yourself.

Ingredients:

8 large red or green peppers
500 g canned tuna
250 g tartare sauce
olive oil
salt

1. *Cut a hole around the stalks of the peppers and remove both the stalks and seeds: try to keep as much of the flesh as possible.*
2. *Mix tuna and tartare sauce together to make a moist stuffing — not too dry but also not so runny that it will all spill out during roasting. Stuff the peppers. Some spillage is permissible; it adds flavour to the sauce.*
3. *Pour oil over the peppers, sprinkle with salt, and roast in a moderate oven (180 °C), basting and turning gently every 15 minutes.*
4. *Serve hot with rice, spooning some of the sauce over the plate. These are also tasty served cold the next day.*

*V*illafranca del Bierzo
June 28

*W*e debated the route out of town. Pete was as usual absolutely confident, and I just argued to keep up appearances.

'Look at the map,' he said, pointing to a 12th century-style aerial photograph.

'That is the route we followed yesterday up to the castle, you donated your knickers to science there, and, ah, this is where we slept.'

'Yes, but, umm, ah.'

'It's all quite simple, we'll just take a short cut down that narrow alley over behind the square and that will lead us down towards the river meeting up with the *Camino* about — here.'

'Which way is up?'

He was right, of course, but it just wasn't natural, this innate sense of direction. It must come from drifting aimlessly around the ocean game-fishing while the rest of us had to work.

We took a circumlocutory route out of the town through a maze of concrete sculpture decorated by graffiti artists. The trail wound through an entire hierarchy of housing estates for employees of the local coal mine. They began with sterile high-rise apartments for the lowest echelon, then terraced housing for the foremen, individual bungalows for the middle management, and finally, the beautifully manicured country estates of the directors. Was this Spain? Every segment appeared to be carefully segregated in strict conformity with the English class system.

After 'Manchester' the scenery became more consistent with my romantic preconceptions of Spain — nostalgia for a world that probably never existed. At the entrance to Prada we saw cows in harness and many large, beautiful family gardens weeded by horse- or cow-drawn ploughs. A factory pickling cherries in *orujo (aguadiente)* provided a welcome diversion and escape from the rain which had been threatening all morning.

In Villafranca, the refuge looked, for want of a better expression, bizarre. Resembling a home-made tunnel house, it was just the sort of thing one could imagine constructed of flotsam and jetsam in the most remote islands of the Pacific. The people were also unusual. We seem to have walked from Manchester to the Appalacian mountains, and stumbled upon hillbillies making moonshine. However, instead of shooting at us, we were invited to help with the pickling of cherries and to sample last year's vintage. They explained: 'Those dammed bureaucrats in the European Community are trying to stop people here distilling *orujo* in the mountains. They won't succeed, of course.'

Unfortunately the *raison d'être* of bureaucrats everywhere is to stop people enjoying themselves. In Galicia the tradition of *orujo* was as important as pigeon to the Basques, and the guitar to Polynesians. *Orujo* is made by distilling the skins and pulp remaining after the fermentation of the red wine. Any wine left over from previous vintages is added to the pot. In France such alcohols are called *marc*, and while the quality is variable, as a general rule the liquor is better in areas where the wines are of poorer calibre. Cognac is a case in point, where the distilled product is of much higher quality than the base wine, and constitutes one of the highest-priced agricultural commodities in the world.

A narrow road wound down the hill to the centre of town past a 15th century castle that had lost two of its towers in the War of Independence against Napoleon. Shutting my eyes, I could imagine the castle under siege: soldiers scaling the walls, the smoke and sound of cannon, the cries and chaos of battle. In the town, many of the houses in the dark, narrow streets still bore coats of arms as reminders of those more turbulent times. Slate roofs, wooden verandas and heavy wooden doors all added to a milieu of mystery. Villafranca del Bierzo was another of the French towns along the road to Santiago, and once boasted two town halls — one for Spaniards and a second for the French.

Back at the ranch, the chief hillbilly, Jesús, seemed quite concerned about my leg. Pete had seen him praying over someone else and asked him to take a look at me. After some indecision about whether to amputate my leg at the knee or slightly above the penis, he began to pray quietly, gently drawing his hands over the leg in downward movements towards the foot, and making ringing and flicking motions with his wrists as if to shake off water. This lasted for about ten minutes and then he asked me to rest for a while. I obeyed, mostly because I was not at all sure I could move. Later he came back and repeated the exercise. Then, shaking his head, he went out into the garden and returned with some fresh arnica foliage. This he moistened with an extract of arnica in alcohol to make a poultice, which he bound tightly around the ankle. He then offered me a glass of *orujo* and cherries; and then another, and another.

'Sit here by the fire and relax.'

No problem, now I *couldn't* move. All I needed was a good cigar.

One young pilgrim looking rather down on his luck — closely resembling Pete and I, in fact — staggered back from a visit to town in a clearly intoxicated state. This was the first time we had ever seen anyone even slightly more than two sheets to windward, and he received a strong ticking off from Jesús for such unacceptable behaviour. It seemed that Jesús acted as a voluntary social worker in addition to his other roles of innkeeper and faith healer.

For the evening meal, Jesus's wife was expecting eight but cheerfully catered for thirty. The atmosphere was festive and high-spirited. Everyone appreciated that this was a special place. To my regret, my Spanish was not good enough to follow the repartee and the stories. At 11 p.m., Pete and I tried to sneak off to bed for an early night, but were sternly ordered back for the *pièce de résistance*, the *queimada*. Jesús was heating up a large earthenware bowl of *orujo* and cherries on the pot-

belly stove. He then set the mixture alight and slowly stirred it for about ten minutes. The lights had been turned off and everyone's attention was drawn to the flickering blue flame hovering above the bowl. Jesús began a mock incantation to cast out the evil spirits of blisters and sore feet. At this point, someone's jeans drying above the stove caught fire. They must have been good quality because they sparkled as they burnt.

Having travelled the greatest distance (it is not possible

to get further away from Spain than New Zealand), it was our duty to taste the cherries first. We then participated with the others until it finally behove us to drain the final droplets from the bowl. *Now* it was time to kip down.

Queimada

To be served only if you are prepared to have your guests stay the night!

Ingredients:

1 lemon
150 g sugar
1 litre brandy

1. *In a large earthenware dish or bowl, place the peel of one lemon and most of the sugar. Heat on the stove.*
2. *Pour over the brandy, reserving a little of the liquor in the bottom of a serving ladle together with the remaining sugar.*
3. *Place the ladle on a hot element and flambé the contents. Introduce the flame into the heated bowl so now the entire mixture is aflame.*
4. *From time to time, stir up the sugar on the bottom so that it all caramelises.*
5. *When the mixture is* au point, *or you can't wait any longer, put out the flame and serve hot.*

Variation: *For a more personalised concoction, add some coffee beans or a liqueur of your choice.*

*G*alicia
June 29

*A*lthough officially we would not reach Galicia until later in the day at El Cebreiro, it seemed that we had already entered a different country. Whereas in Castilla, life had seemed a vain struggle against the dust, here the landscape was spring-cleaned daily. We were now walking through forests of oaks, poplars and very old chestnuts, some with diameters up to 2 metres.

It was raining continually, but the droplet size was minute. It was like walking through fog, and we were not really getting wet. Nonetheless, Pete pulled a light raincoat from his pack.

'Hey, what was all that sanctimonious babble about having faith in God and not needing a raincoat.'

'Oh, I was referring to you. You don't think I'd be silly enough to walk across Spain without some protection from the rain?'

The rivers looked clean, and if it had been warmer it would have been tempting to go for a swim. Inevitably there was plastic litter, although less here than on some other parts of the walk. For all that, it seemed all the more obtrusive. It is a shame that, despite a consumer society of some 40 million people, Spain sometimes continues to have the same philosophy towards rubbish as a medieval village. Mind you, rubbish excepted, the olden-world charms and virtues were amongst the most enjoyble aspects of this pilgrimage.

The topography became more and more rugged, and we were often in forest. The atmosphere reminded me of the French Pyrénées although the villages seemed older. The lanes through the villages were awash with water and mud. Women wore prehistoric rugby boots: wooden clogs with two very characteristic sprigs under the heel and ball of the foot — quite useful in the mud. The houses were of stone construction with slate roofs. Livestock were commonly stabled under the family home and fed with hay that had been scythed and then dried in characteristic conical-shaped haystacks in the fields. The refuse was subsequently mucked out to be used as fertiliser on small plots of vegetables.

My shin had greatly improved and was quite comfortable as long as I kept walking — each time we stopped it would seize up and then take a kilometre or so before it would begin to move freely once more. The temperature was wonderful for hiking, and we both felt terrific. The rain was heavier, and we were now walking in low cloud through which we could only vaguely distinguish the forms of the hills. We were above the bush-line, and the vegetation was heather and low scrub. Cowbells sounded as foghorns above the surge of cascading water, and very occasionally we would catch a vague glimpse of animals on the skyline. Finally, in complete mist, and almost by accident, we fell upon El Cebreiro. It was very, very cold, and almost impossible to see anything; it seemed that we were stranded here for the night.

Pilgrims have been passing by El Cebreiro, perched at 1300 metres between two kingdoms, since the 9th century. The village preserves some original thatched Celtic cottages, in which it is possible to see how, for warmth, the bedrooms were located above the stable. My son still uses the same technique, and much to his mother's disgust insists on sleeping with his dog.

The church was a lovely combination of wood and stone construction. According to tradition, it was the scene of a miracle towards the end of the 12th century. After a winter storm that engulfed the villages with snow up to the roofs of the houses and isolated the region from the outside world, a shepherd from a neighbouring village continued to make the journey each day to celebrate mass. The monk officiating had little faith and thought, 'He must be so stupid to make the journey for so little bread and wine.'

Then, before their very eyes, the bread was miraculously transformed into real flesh and the wine to real blood.

Some years later, but long before all souvenirs were made in Taiwan, Queen Isabelle passed this way en route to Santiago, and took a fancy to the chalice and plate. She would have liked to take them with her, but was thwarted by her mule, which absolutely refused to budge. This was interpreted as another divine sign, and the 12th century chalice and plate are still to be seen on display. Before them, we prayed for family and friends, giving thanks for the intercessions in Villafranca and the cure of my leg.

The above example of a cynical priest whose lack of faith is contrasted with that of a simple peasant serves as a recurring theme in medieval literature, as shown by the following story adapted from that of Jean Bodel in a collection of morality tales and fables — *Fabliaux et Contes du Moyen Age.*[15] It begins thus:

> *To amuse you a little I will recount a story of a poor peasant. It is the truth, I promise — I'm not about to tell you any falsehoods. Now on the day of the Feast of the Virgin, this peasant and his wife went to pray at the church. From the pulpit, the priest explained God's sincere promise to repay in double to those who give with a joyous and willing heart.*
>
> *'As anyone with half an eye can see, it is rewarding to give out of love for God.'*
>
> *'Hey, did you hear what he just said?' whispered the old villain, nudging his wife in the ribs. 'If we give with a willing heart, God will give us back twice as much. What do you think about giving our cow to the priest? — for the love of God of course! She is no bloody use, doesn't give hardly any milk.'*
>
> *His wife was of a like mind.*
>
> *'In its present condition, I'd rather he had it,' she affirmed.*
>
> *And so it came to pass that soon after chapel, the husband returned to the church, leading the cow by its halter. This he presented to the priest exclaiming that they were giving Blérain, for that was its name, for the love of God, and vowing that she was no longer theirs.*
>
> *'Friend, you have acted wisely,' exclaimed the wily priest, who thought of nothing except accumulating wealth. 'Go, you must do as your conscience dictates.'*
>
> *As the old man departed, the priest thought, 'If all my parishioners were as wise as that idiot, what a splendid herd I should soon have!'*
>
> *The sacristan was ordered to take Blérain out to pasture and to leave her tethered with the priest's own cow. This he did. Left to their own devices, the priest's cow lowered its head so as to graze, but Blérain would have none of it: she pulled and pulled so strongly on the rope that the other had no choice but to follow her out of the meadow. Blérain towed the other cow bellowing loudly and protesting across farm and field until they both eventually found their way back to the home of the peasant. There waiting was the scallywag, overcome with joy.*
>
> *'Wife,' he called. 'It is true that God repays in double. Blérain has returned with another: she has brought back a huge brown cow. Our stable will be full!'*

This story shows how foolish are those without faith. Good comes to those to whom God gives and not to those who hoard or hide what they have. Since no-one can profit except with a large measure of luck, it is by pure chance that the peasant ends up with two cows while the priest loses all. He who seeks to advance, loses ground. Thus is the way of the world.

So may the God, whose goodness exceeds all understanding, protect from evil all those who have heard this story and he who has recounted it. And now, comrades, if it so pleases you, find me something to drink!

Whether the clergy were, in fact, as avaricious or as licentious as is often depicted in these stories, I'm not certain. That evening we ate with three priests from San Sebastian, who were travelling to Santiago by car, and, who I am delighted to report, gave no cause for alarm. They had voracious appetites, but then so did we, and the competition for the chips was fierce. The food was the best we'd had for several days and, although young, the wine was also passable.

*C*onejo con Kumara

Rabbit with Sweet Potato

Kumara (sweet potato) has a wonderful nutty flavour and its possibilities are underutilised in New Zealand cuisine. Here it serves as a substitute for chestnuts in this Galician dish.

Ingredients:

2 rabbits	saffron
salt	1 cup brandy
oil	1 cup dry sherry
250 g ham	1 cup chicken stock
1 onion	1 Tblsp cornflour
2 cloves garlic	500 g peeled kumara or sweet
2 carrots	potato

1. *Wash the rabbits, cut up into serving portions, and season with salt.*
2. *Brown the meat over a vigorous heat in heavy-bottomed pan.*
3. *Pour the meat and oil into an earthenware casserole dish. Add the ham cut up into small pieces, together with a finely chopped onion, crushed garlic, sliced carrots and the saffron.*
4. *Add brandy, sherry and enough stock to cover the meat. A little cornflour mixed in cold water will help thicken the sauce. Cook together for 45 minutes.*
5. *Add the kumara at this point and top up with more liquid (stock or water) if necessary. Continue cooking for another 20 or 25 minutes until the kumara have softened. Serve hot.*

𝒯riacastela
June 30

𝒯he descent from El Cebreiro took place in fog and light rain. Since no part of my body was complaining too much, the *bota* was empty, and the scenery not particularly exhilarating, I mused ineffectually on the vexed question of whether Jews had been given a choice; that is to say, whether or not the death of Jesus was inevitable and, if God was all-knowing, what significance had free will?

Except for acknowledging the fact that Jesus willingly participated in both an illegal arrest and a mock trial, I made little progress. The behaviour of the Jewish authorities was, of course, predictable: bureaucrats would always opt for the status quo even in the face of Messianic miracles, and God would surely have realised this long before Jesus. There are other examples of this in Jewish history, as indicated by the following account of a doctrinal argument around the end of the first century AD between Rabbi Eliezer ben Hyrcanus and his colleagues. The story, as described by Geza Vermes, goes thus:

> *Having exhausted his arsenal of reasoning and still not convinced them, he performed a miracle only to be told that there was no room for miracles in legal debate. In exasperation he then exclaimed: 'If my teaching is correct, may it be proved by Heaven!' Whereupon a celestial voice declared: 'What have you against Rabbi Eliezer, for his teaching is correct?' But this intervention was ruled out of order because in the Bible it is written that decisions are to be reached by majority vote.*[16]

Difficult questions! But then as witnessed by one Zophar the Naamathite: 'Can you probe the limits of the Almighty? What can you do?'[17]

At this point I also received a celestial message in the form of a random synaptic misfire into the cranial void: 'I'm getting rather bored with these theosophical ramblings. Just shut up and walk, for God's sake!'

$\mathscr{P}$lato Escocés Hecho con Vísceras de Oveja y Avena

Haggis

It has been remarked already that the insides of animals are treasured in Spain. Haggis has the simple virtue that you get most of the guts in one go and it's great fun to prepare. Basically, it comprises the heart, liver and lungs, all cooked and mashed up with oatmeal, stuffed into the stomach, and the whole caboodle boiled for several hours. Scottish tradition dictates that the haggis is then stabbed with a dirk by a man wearing a dress, all to the poetry of Robbie Burns and the wailing of bagpipes. Since the Galicians are also a Celtic people there is undoubtedly a Spanish equivalent to haggis; there certainly is in Creole cooking, which has Spanish cuisine as part of its pedigree.

Ingredients:

For the haggis:	large pinch cayenne pepper
1 sheep's stomach	juice of 1 lemon
1 sheep's heart	$^{1}/_{2}$ tsp nutmeg
1 sheep's liver	
1 sheep's lungs, with windpipe	*For the clapshot:*
2 to 4 onions	500 g potatoes
125 g beef suet	500 g white turnips
300 g fine oatmeal	1 Tblsp chives
1 heaped tsp salt	1 Tblsp butter
$^{1}/_{2}$ tsp pepper	salt and pepper

1. *Wash and thoroughly clean the sheep's stomach. Soak overnight in the fridge in several changes of strongly salted cold water. Drain.*
2. *Wash and clean the heart, liver, lungs and windpipe. Place them in a*

large pot containing boiling water. Hang the windpipe over the side so that one end is in the pot and the other in a basin of water; it acts as a drain to remove the blood and frothy material that rises to the surface. Drink a glass of whisky. Boil the organs for 2 hours. Allow to cool.

3. *Mince the cold, cooked organs. Parboil the onions, mince them and add to the meat along with the beef suet, lightly toasted oatmeal, salt, pepper and cayenne pepper. Stir in 600 ml of the bouillon, lemon juice and nutmeg. Mix well.*

4. *Have another whisky, then half fill the sheep's stomach with the minced meat. Squeeze the air out of the other half; this empty portion allows room for the oatmeal to expand. Sew up the stomach and prick it well so that air can escape — an explosion at this point would mean redecorating the kitchen. Put the stomach into boiling water, let it come back to the boil, and simmer for 3 hours. Prick occasionally during cooking. Drink a glass of whisky — just a wee dram!*

5. *To make the clapshot, boil the potatoes and turnips together, mash with the chives and butter, then season to taste.*

6. *Serve the haggis and clapshot together, with small glasses of neat whisky to drink between mouthfuls.*

The Path to Portomarin

July 1

*W*e spent a relaxed morning waiting for the shops to open. I found a nice lightweight (weight still being a major concern) woollen jersey, and an even lighter raincoat only two or three sizes too small. Then began a glorious carefree ramble along stone-lined lanes traversing a countryside dotted with small farming hamlets, the walking made all the more pleasant by the happy conjunction of weather and distance from responsibilities.

There was water everywhere and the paths had become small rivers. My boots were supreme; the pain of the previous four weeks forgotten, I splashed with flourish through mud, slush, and liquefied cow-shit. And to think I had once been on the verge of throwing them out just because of a few trivial blisters. We actually saw some old women wearing very similar footwear.

'You would have been right up to date with the fashions in about 1920,' remarked Pete.

Little did he know that in my family, clothes were handed down for generations. Come to think of it, right now I could do with my father's old oilskin. One generation later, coats like his have become fashionable items amongst yuppies in Auckland and Sydney. One can't be seen dressed inappropriately in a Range Rover in the centre of the city — heaven forbid! According to a friend, it was even possible in London to buy spray-on mud for added authenticity. That wouldn't have sold very well in Galicia.

We overtook a family with three very young children — the husband ineffectually struggling with a baby in a pushchair. The tiny wheels were awash in a river of flowing mud as the pushchair was desperately manoeuvred to avoid being broached by the tidal stream. Pete helped them through the worst part, but it was hard to imagine how they would cope for the rest of the day — divorce seemed inevitable. Later in Portomarin we would find them in a bar celebrating their day's accomplishments, justifiably proud of their seven-year-old daughter who had walked all day without complaining. Their family pilgrimage to the tomb of Saint James by car was an annual event, but since this was a

Jubilee year, they had decided to undertake the voyage by foot.

Several kilometres outside of Portomarin we saw a young boy, with an English-style cheese cutter cap, resting on a stone fence. He, the fields, and a blue sky littered with puffy white patches, conjured up the image of a Constable watercolour. I should have liked to take a photograph, but thanks to Pancho, bless his tortured soul, I could not. The boy turned out to be a rather attractive young woman.

'Where have you come from?' she asked in Spanish.

'*Oloron en Francia.*'

'No, I mean, from what country are you?'

'*Nueva Zelanda.*'

'Ah, New Zealand.'

Maggie was Dutch and this was her first day of walking. She was a bit uncertain whether she could walk the 100 kilometres to Santiago. We described the range of people we had met on the trip and how few were such finely tuned athletes as now stood before her.

'Don't worry,' said Pete, 'everyone agrees that the first four weeks are the worst.'

And with those words of comfort, we carried on towards Portomarin.

At Portomarin, the auberge was full with groups of school-children. We looked so down-cast that the lady found us a couple of beds in a small room to ourselves. Maggie arrived not long after, and since it was her 21st birthday, we went for a drink together and eventually a meal — a some-what disappointing paella. Paella is basically a rice and sea-food dish that originates from Valencia and which has be-come part of the national and

international repertoire, a gastronomic symbol for the whole of Spain.

Maggie was an anthropology student and had recently finished a research project investigating religious ideas in a small village near Salamanca in the south of Spain. She had become interested in the conflict of ideas created by the introduction into the village of a spiritual renewal process called 'the new path'. This 'cult', which had the support of the village priest and the Pope, was aimed at enlivening the Catholic church and was creating some tension in the village between the older people, and younger, more charismatic members of the flock struggling to explore how Christianity could work in their lives. Traditionally, church here was for women over 50 and not at all for men. Where was it any different?

For many of the older people, brought up in an era when mass was conducted in Latin and which few of them understood, the Virgin remained a more relevant religious figure than Jesus. They were aware of the presence of the Almighty, but the Virgin was the closest tangible manifestation of His presence. The priest, who was tolerated for his position, and resented because he was Basque, said that they were not real Christians. The younger charismatics, many of whom had had some recent trauma in their lives, such as the loss of jobs or the death of loved ones, spent time singing songs of praise, reading the Bible and trying to relate its message to their everyday lives. To their older protagonists, more inured to the whims of fate, this was completely incomprehensible.

'They say they talk with God, but how can you talk with the wind?'

I was also interested in Maggie's comment that many of the old homes in the village were being bought as holiday cottages by the rich. This was preserving the buildings, but undoubtedly introducing other tensions and change in the fabric of life in a village where the average age was 70 and where it was common to meet people in their 90s. We had become aware of how elderly people continued to pursue active social lives. Bars always had several tables of old men in berets playing cards or dominos, usually smoking cigars and enjoying a drink. Older women were less conspicuous in the bars but were still to be seen in the streets.

$\mathcal{A}$rroz con Pollo
Chicken with Rice

This simplified but tasty, colourful alternative to paella can be found on the menus of most restaurants in Spain.

Ingredients:

1 chicken	¹/₄ cup olive oil
2 cups water	1 green pepper
¹/₂ cup white wine	1 red pepper
2 tsp salt	1 onion, extra
¹/₂ onion	2 cloves garlic
1 bunch parsley	2 very ripe tomatoes
1 carrot	200 g shelled peas
1 stick celery	2 heaped cups rice
1 pinch saffron	salt and pepper
2 Tblsp flour	parsley

1. *Cut the chicken into pieces, place in a casserole dish and cover with water and wine. Season with 2 tsp salt.*
2. *Add the half onion, parsley, carrot and celery. Cook over a moderate heat for about 30 minutes.*
3. *Take out the chicken. Strain liquid; leave to cool, and then spoon off as much fat as is possible. Add saffron, return to the boil, and leave just simmering on low heat.*
4. *Roll the pieces of chicken in seasoned flour and brown in hot oil in a large frying pan. Take out of pan and put to one side.*
5. *Add more oil and fry sliced peppers for a few minutes. Throw in the finely chopped extra onion and crushed garlic and continue frying until the onions are translucent. Now add peeled and chopped tomatoes and the peas, and fry the mixture all together for 3 to 4 minutes. Add the rice and swirl around in the oil and vegetables, coating the grains with the sauce. Now pour in the cooled bouillon, bring back to the boil, cover,*

lower heat, and simmer together for 10 minutes.

6. *Check the seasoning and then add the chicken and cook another 10 minutes until the rice has absorbed most of the liquid and the chicken is tender. Sprinkle with parsley and allow to stand a few minutes uncovered before serving.*

ℒeboreiro
July 2

𝒯here was little of interest early in the day. It was an empty land-scape dominated by weeds and scrub-like species of broom, gorse and heather, against which some isolated pockets of forestry made little impression. The sky looked forbidding — dreadful in fact. It was 11 a.m. before we could find somewhere to have breakfast — Galicia had quite ruined my statistics of the number of bars per family, it really was another country.

After a cheese sandwich, which took more effort to chew than walking 20 kilometres, we chatted with another pilgrim, Enrique, on leave from the Guardia Civil. In his hostel in Portomarin it had been almost impossible to sleep because of a school group from Andulucía, excited after their first day's walking. They had sung and played guitars most of the night. When Enrique complained that, having walked from the French border, he deserved more consideration, they had replied with some surprise, 'But in Andulucía, only the dead sleep!'

We saw many more horse-drawn wooden ploughs in use and later

watched two men weeding a several hectare paddock of potatoes with such a plough drawn by two cows. I wouldn't have believed it was possible to do this so effectively without the animals trampling all over the plants. One man led and another guided the plough behind. Pete was impressed, but not completely convinced: 'I think I'll stick with my tractor.'

At Arzúa, we caught up with Maggie and continued walking together. She talked more about her studies and an interview which she was about to publish about a refugee in Holland. This boy had spent his first few years in Eritrea, including three months in the desert as his family moved about to avoid the war. His recollections of that time are few, but he remembers how proud his grandfather was of him when he gave up his turn on the camel for his sisters, and also how he was scolded when, with the enthusiasm typical of small boys, he would run to touch the very occasional tree.

'Take it easy, you must conserve your strength.'

The family then spent the next five years in the Sudan living on a government farm for refugees. This enjoyable experience was abruptly terminated when his father, who had been working in Saudi Arabia, returned and took him back to live with him. There, life was dreadful — his brothers were cruel and he had to adapt to a fundamentalist Arab education system. At 13, he and another brother escaped to Holland, where he now lives with foster parents. He has done very well at school, but has problems: he feels that he can adopt any one of several personalities, each of which reflect various facets of past experience, but he can not be sure which is the real him. (I knew how he felt.) His foster parents think that it is now time for him to move out and make his own way, but according to the statistics, very few of these refugee children can deal successfully with the extreme changes demanded of them.

We arrived in Leboreiro — the country of hares. I had not noticed any game, but the very thought of hares evoked memories of Pierrette's hare liver terrine, and with those thoughts came the realisation that I was hungry — we hadn't eaten anything since that cheese sandwich.

I bought some groceries from a very old bar. Short of cash, it was necessary to be careful. That wasn't too difficult; the shop hadn't been provisioned for some centuries and I bought an assortment of tinned foods left over from the Spanish Civil War. The owner insisted that I try his wine. It was dreadful.

'It is wonderful,' I said diplomatically, 'but my friends don't drink.'

He didn't know where anything was.

'I'm a farmer, a man of the land, not a shopkeeper.'

'Have you any bread?'

'Well there doesn't seem to be any, can you see it? No, well, probably my wife has some in the fridge.'

She had and he cut me off a few slices.

At the refuge, three Spanish families had arrived. We had been nodding acquaintances for several days. Despite suffering dreadfully from blisters and sore legs they were still all very cheerful. They immediately endeared themselves to us by swapping some of our instant coffee for a glass of Cointreau — a reminder of the miracle of Jesus turning water into wine. They then went out singing something that sounded like flamenco. They were still singing on their return an hour or so later, and we were invited to join them for cheese, bread and *empanada* — the Galician version of a Cornish pasty. They were from Algeciras in the south of Andulucía. As usual, it was Pete who made their acquaintance. By the time they had appreciated that we were from New Zealand, and this often took some considerable time, had marvelled at the photo album, the beauty of his wife and the size of Pete's family — '*Uno, dos, tres, cuatro, cinco, seis, siete — siete! ¡Dios mió!*' — we were all firm friends. We finished two small bottles of *orujo*, one having been a gift from the hillbillies of Villafranca.

Paco began to sing — an ancient Andulucían song describing the feelings of the last Moorish general as he was driven out of Granada in 1492, the last Arab toehold in Spain. As he left the castle of the Alhambra for the final time, tears welled in his eyes. The song describes the amazement of the general's wife at the sight of her husband crying while he explains how he had fought many battles in his career, winning some and losing others, but now he felt as if he was having to leave his soul here in Spain. Flamenco can make most other music seem frivolous and the emotion in Paco's voice was enough to make anyone cry.

Paco explained how flamenco must be sung from the heart.

'It cannot be learnt like the guitar or dance, one is either born with the skill or not, and then it must be fostered in the streets.'

Apparently there were some forty different types of flamenco and we heard many different examples. As Paco sang, the others clapped and Pepe-Luis embellished the basic rhythms by tapping with his knuckles and fingers on the table. The emotion and intensity with which they felt their culture is amazing. Despite their blisters and pain, when Paco began to sing *sevillanas*, the girls rose and began to dance, slowly at first, and then faster as the tempo increased. All the men were singing now: fiesta time.

$\mathscr{T}$errine de Liebre
Hare Liver Terrine

As a tribute to Leboreiro, we offer this recipe adapted from the kitchen of Jean-Pierre's family, who would normally use venison liver. I'm sure that one could find similar examples in Spanish country kitchens.

Ingredients:

300 to 400 g hare liver	$^1/_2$ cup cognac
300 g good quality mince	1 tsp dried, chopped sage
500 g boned and trimmed pork belly	1 Tblsp finely chopped parsley
	1 Tblsp dried or fresh thyme
a handful of bread soaked in milk	bacon rashers
	1 heaped tsp salt
1 medium-sized onion	lard
2 eggs	

1. *Place the liver, mince, and half of the pork in a mixing bowl. Add the milk-moistened bread after lightly squeezing. Add the remaining ingredients (with the exception of the rest of the pork, lard and bacon rashers) and blend finely.*
2. *Roughly dice the remaining pork and fold into the blended mixture. This will give the terrine a more interesting texture.*
3. *Line the base of a bread tin with a thin layer of melted lard. Add the terrine mixture and cover with rashers of bacon. Pour a very thin layer of melted lard over the top.*
4. *Bake for $1^1/_2$ hours in the oven at 160 °C.*
5. *Leave to cool before eating.*

*A*rca?
July 3

*M*aggie decided to detour at Mellid and visit a monastery about a day's march off the direct route to Santiago. Having proved she could walk as well as anyone, she wanted to earn her arrival in Santiago. I was tempted to go with her: the closer we got to Santiago, the faster we walked, and the less I wanted this experience to be over. However, to spin the journey out seemed a bit artificial and so after some discussion, Pete and I decided to continue.

By 9 a.m. we were already in Mellid and the town was getting ready for its fiesta. Octopus was being prepared in the street in large copper vessels on open fires. First they scrubbed the skin from the head with

a pot scrubber. Some recipes require the octopus to be tenderised by bashing it forcefully against rocks, but whether this had been the case here I'm not sure. Anyway, then the whole octopuses are boiled furiously in salted water for one or more hours until tender. Drained, left to cool and then cut up into slices with sharp scissors, they are eaten with a dressing of olive oil and a garnish of finely chopped, mild red pepper. Pete and I tried some accompanied by bread and a large bowl of a very agreeable red wine. It was very nice, although personally I prefer octopus when it retains a bit more of its texture like calamari or abalone (paua for Kiwis).

The bar in Mellid was very simple with no concessions to decor. An occasional bare light bulb was separated from a sagging ceiling by exposed wires. A large fireplace had almost burnt through the chimney and the surrounding ceiling was heavily scorched. The tables were simple trestles covered with white paper, and the floor was covered with sawdust. It was absolutely fantastic! Sometimes it seems to me that the more run-down the establishment the better the food. If that isn't always true, then perhaps the converse is.

Before Maggie left we decided on a group photograph in front of the fountain. That wasn't as simple as it sounded. No-one would take a photograph for us. The camera was viewed with as much suspicion as a bomb. The Andalucíans were amazed, and as my mum would have said, 'There is none so queer as folk.'

Finally a young boy was embarrassed into taking the camera, pressing the button only with great trepidation and after first shutting his eyes as if to prepare himself for the forthcoming explosion.

Maggie left us at this point as the rest of us forced our way through the throng of country folk from surrounding villages who had come for the fiesta and to sell their cheeses and bread, lace and other crafts. It was very hot. Leaving the village, we strolled along country lanes through forests of birch, eucalyptus, and oak. Except for the occasional Romanesque bridge and women doing their washing in streams, we could have been in New Zealand.

We rested next at an ancient stone building that had once been a hospital for pilgrims in the Middle Ages and that had recently been restored and converted into an auberge. A lovely single-arched stone bridge led to it across a river. This time the water was irresistible and I plunged in. Cold-gasping purgative shocks gradually gave way to tingling muscles, anaesthetised limbs and sedated blisters. I drifted lazily, a sun-flecked, goose-bumped corpse, savouring each painfree moment.

Pepe and Paco's wives were both suffering quite badly with sore legs and so the Guardia Civil took them ahead in a Land Rover to Arca.

'It's only fifteen kilometres,' they had announced casually before leaving.

Somewhat later, taking coffee after lunch in Arzúa, we enquired as to the distance to Arca — or was it Varca — no-one was too sure: this village didn't feature on any of our maps.

'Oh, about twenty-five kilometres,' said the barman, expansively.

Too expansively in our opinion.

'Rubbish!' exclaimed everyone, as if this would somehow shorten the distance.

It did!

'Oh well, perhaps it is closer to eighteen.'

'Boof!'

'Maybe fifteen?'

'OK.'

We continued on towards Arca or Varca. Paco and Pepe were becoming increasingly distraught at the prospects of ever finding their wives. They set a blistering pace. Some 5 kilometres later I asked an old man for general directions. His reply was all but drowned out by Paco and Pepe.

'How far to Arca?' Pepe interrupted, almost screaming.

'Oh about twenty-eight or twenty-nine kilometres.'

We didn't even bother to acknowledge his response.

The pace increased, Paco and Pepe in the lead. I wasn't sure I could keep this up. The lunchtime coffee was having its usual diuretic effect and Paco stepped discretely behind a tree. He was very close to a fence, I just hoped it wasn't electrified. He and Pepe soon disappeared in the distance. With their single-minded determination to find their wives, they reminded me of Pizarro marching across South America oblivious to mountains, mosquitos, Indians or mud. *Toda por la patria* had become *Toda por la familia.*

Several hours later, Arca was as elusive as ever. Reminiscent of our entrance into Burgos, it was always: 'Only another three kilometres.'

Finally the impossible happened and we arrived. After correcting for Spanish relativistic effects, various quantum phenomena overlooked by Einstein, and the effects of the wine at lunch, it seemed that it was about 24 kilometres from Arzúa, more or less what the barman had initially told us. Since lunch, we had walked at 6 kilometres an hour for four hours over broken terrain and were absolutely exhausted.

Our friends seemed a little out of sorts. I recognised the signs — my mother used to display the same symptoms when as children, either I, or more frequently one of my sisters, would arrive home late. While waiting she would work herself up into a frenzy imagining all sorts of bizarre and horrific possibilities such as murder, rape, mayhem, black magic or just a plain ordinary kidnapping — things largely unheard of in those days in New Zealand but which the tabloid press would have us believe were commonplace overseas. When we finally arrived home, her relief would give way to anger and the wrath of God would fall upon us as we were belted all the way to our bedrooms. My children complain that such irrationality seems to be genetic. Not tortured with Irish imaginations, the Andalucíans recovered their normal high spirits without any blood-letting, and in time for a drink and a quick meal of chips, eggs and salad.

*C*alamares Guisados
Squid Stew

Stuffed baby squid cooked in their ink (*calamares en su tinta*) is another speciality dish found along coastal regions of southern Europe. Here is a much simpler but tasty variation on a Galician theme.

Ingredients:

2 kg large calamari	1 green pepper
olive oil	2 cloves garlic
1¹/₂ kg potatoes cut into cubes	660 ml chicken stock
2 onions	1 cup white wine
3 tomatoes	olive oil for frying
1 red pepper	salt and pepper

1. *Clean squid well and then slice them.*
2. *In a large frying pan, heat oil and fry potatoes until golden. Take out of pan and place to one side.*
3. *Chop and lightly fry the onions, tomatoes, peppers and garlic.*
4. *Add squid and when these have become soft (after only a few minutes), add back the fried potatoes. Add stock and wine to just cover other ingredients.*
5. *Simmer on low heat for 1 hour, adding more stock as required to maintain the level of liquid.*
6. *Season to taste and serve.*

ℛendezvous in Santiago de Compostela

July 4

𝒫rogress was slow. Exhausted after yesterday's effort, Paco held tightly to his wife's hand — we would not have a repeat of yesterday's fiasco. At Monxoi (Mount Joy in English) an immense village catering for 800 people had been built in the expectation of pilgrims coming for the Holy Day in three weeks. Here, giving thanks to God, pilgrims throughout the centuries were at last able to see the towers of the cathedral of Compostela in the distance. From this point some pilgrims would walk the remaining few kilometres barefoot.

Our friends decided to stay overnight and rest. With the ball in hand, and being so close to the goal posts, Pete and I were now impatient to finish.

We were within five minutes of the cathedral walking up a cobblestone road, when we suddenly heard a very familiar *sevillana* above the sound of an equally familiar diesel engine.

'Alex!'

We helped him unload the Rioja from the boot, and shortly after we were all sitting down together in a restaurant with Hema, Valvenera and Adrián swapping stories over a flaming bowl of *café con aguardiente*. Alex was trading with the owner reserve Rioja for seafood specialities, including a delicious plate of grilled mussels in a spicy sauce, while Hema and Valvanera, to the applause of the entire restaurant, sang the song which they had composed en route.

Adrián recounted his experiences in Villafranca, where he too had been treated by the chief hillbilly. That time, the healing had been unsuccessful. However, also in the refuge that night had been a monk — a young man — who usually lived as a hermit in a cave outside of Barcelona eating only vegetables, and spending his life in prayer. Placing his finger inside the blister, he asked Adrián to concentrate. Adrián felt absolutely nothing, despite having had so much pain a few moments earlier that he thought he may not have been able to complete the pilgrimage. The next day Adrián walked without pain.

'Villafranca is a very spiritual place.'

I commented that the people in Galicia in the countryside seemed to be more suspicious of strangers than in other parts of the Camino.

'Ah, you know that they are a Celtic people?'

It was true, their music was almost as good as that of the Irish and Scots, and their wine, almost as bad.

Alex and Adrián arranged a room for Pete and I in a *fonda*, or a small family-run hotel, in the old part of the city so that we could get to the church early and without packs. Alex was keen to do a last round of the

bars and I improved my reputation by finding a mildewy establishment operated by a barman of decrepit complexion. The wine was excellent, and a large pot of soup slowly simmering over onto the stove behind the bar added to the ambience. Comfortably ensconced in this bar, we were close to Cape Finisterre, the so-called 'end-of-the-earth'. Pre-Columbus we would have been separated by only a few nautical miles of water from an underworld inhabited by unimaginable monsters, artists' impressions of which are still to be seen in the colourful and horrific borders of early navigational charts.

The evening finished with a plate of fried, small, spicy green peppers from Padrón, the site of the supposed landing of the boat carrying Saint James to Galicia after his execution by Herod.

$\mathcal{M}$ejillones Cantabria
Cantabrian Grilled Mussels

A bit of fuss, but this tasty plate from the Cantabrian coast is very easy and well worth the effort.

Ingredients:

3 kg mussels in their shells	1 cup dry white wine
butter	2 fresh bay leaves
1 large red pepper	1 small hot chilli pepper
1 large green pepper	1 tsp paprika
6 small onions	saffron
3 cloves garlic	lemon juice
3 tomatoes	breadcrumbs
salt	parsley

1. *Scrape the mussel shells clean with a knife under fresh water. Place in a large, covered pan, add just a little water or white wine to cover the bottom, and steam open the shellfish.*
2. *As soon as the mussels have opened take them out — extra cooking will only make them tough. Preserve the juice and set the mussels to one side. When they have cooled a little, discard the top shell and arrange mussels side by side in a single layer in a baking tray.*
3. *To prepare the sauce, heat the butter in a heavy frypan and fry the diced peppers for a couple of minutes before adding the onions and crushed garlic. Continue frying for another 3 or 4 minutes over high heat, stirring so that the onions don't catch. Then add the peeled and finely chopped tomatoes. Season very slightly with salt — the juice from the mussels, which will be added later, is very salty! Simmer uncovered until the tomatoes release their juice.*
4. *Add the wine, bay leaves, the hot pepper and paprika. Leave simmering for a further 15 minutes.*
5. *Add saffron and a cup of the juice from the mussels and boil for 5 minutes.*

6. *Pour the sauce over the mussels, sprinkle with breadcrumbs and place under the grill.*
7. *Once the 'sauce' has browned, moisten with lemon juice and baptise with chopped parsley. Serve immediately.*

ℛedemption?

July 5

𝒥ust behind the cathedral we were reconciled with Paco and the rest of our friends from Algeceras. In fact, almost everyone was here except the kindly gentleman with the heart condition and his wife. There were the three girls from Seville, a Brazilian surfer, Javier from Bilbao, José and Maria from León, and Enrique of the Guardia Civil, all queuing to receive Certificates of Pilgrimage, a Compostela, a guarantee in Latin of having walked more than 150 kilometres.

We all visited the cathedral together and in turn ritualistically placed our fingers at the base of the sculptured Tree of Jesse in the five hollows worn away by the touch of millions of earlier pilgrims. A fabulous integration of Old and New Testament themes, this portal was executed by one Maestro Mateo between 1168 and 1188. As described by Mabille de Poncheville, Christ sits above the principal entrance for the pilgrims, and in the imagery of John's revelationary vision of the Apocalypse, he is surrounded by a semi-circle of the Elders and Angels, his hands open for prayer and ready to receive his flock.[18] At his feet and at the summit of the Tree of Jesse, the column around which interlaces Christ's earthy genealogy, Saint James presents a radiant welcome to pilgrims; he is no longer on horseback but in simple robes, and with his pilgrim's staff he resembles those whom he is receiving. At a more humble rung, at the very base of the column, is the sculptor himself, kneeling andtouching his chest with his right hand

and 'leaving us uncertain as to whether he is claiming responsibility for his hymn of stone or only recognising his right in the place of a Samaritan in the edifice embellished by him.'

Again according to Mabille de Poncheville, the tradition of touching the kneeling Maestro Mateo extends back to artisans amongst the pilgrims. These had a particular veneration for the author of this miracle of sculpture before which they would prostrate themselves on arrival.

'It was as if by the warmth of the human touch, he would be able to communicate the secrets of his beautiful work as they asked for a small portion of his inspiration. The popular name of the architect in Galician is *O Santo Dos Croqués*, the Saint of Blows, by reason of the caresses he receives on his head.'

We then filed past the silver bust of Saint James behind the alter, embracing him from behind and making a quick prayer before taking the stairs down to the narrow crypt beneath the alter to see the tomb of the apostle. Despite the beauty of the church and its turbulent history, I felt a slight malaise — it was all strangely anticlimactic and I was missing the daily routine of walking, which had become strangely addictive. Perhaps, as with many other things, it was the doing that was more important than the ending.

The church was full of tourists who had made the pilgrimage by coach, car or aeroplane. Instead of smelling of sweat and unwashed underpants, the air reeked of Chanel No. 5 and cologne. It was impossible to find a seat; walkers may have had priority in the refuges but this was clearly not the case in the cathedral. Heretics!

As might be expected when you get a thousand or so Spaniards together, the singing in the mass was wonderful. The highlight for the tourists was the spectacular swinging of the gigantic silver incense burner, the *botafumeiro*. This is the size of a man and is raised by a rope and pulley system operated by seven acolytes in black and scarlet robes, and then, once lit, set in motion. As the acolytes pull in unison, the swing is amplified further and further, and with each successive pull on the ropes the burner swings higher and higher, whooshing laterally across the nave of the church trailing flames and smoke, the fragrance of the incense overwhelming the aroma of dirty underwear, sweaty armpits and Chanel No. 5. When the rope finally touches the perimeter of the upper dome of the church, the amplitude is dampened until the burner sinks back to earth to mark the completion of the service. It is said that the *botafumeiro* fell once, before Catherine of Aragon on her wedding voyage to Henry VIII and England. She should have accepted the warning.

There had also been the opportunity to participate in the Eucharist. When, as the result of pressure from the rest of my family, I first began attending services, handcuffed to the pews of our local Anglican church, communion was the only part of the service that held any appeal. The liturgy was beautiful and the wine and wafers represented a welcome relief from the dreary hymns — a sort of confessional half-time ritual. With the passage of time and increasing understanding of its biblical significance, communion eventually became a personal high point of the service. Although the liturgy in the Catholic church is almost identical, communion itself is often a more perfunctory affair. Perhaps it is because only the clergy get to sup the wine, a flagrant example of the clergy pulling rank — a totally unjustified reward for celibacy.

In Zaragoza, Blanca had asked me if Protestants believe that the communion wine and bread are really the blood and flesh of Christ. My view is that they are both symbolic, and their significance is to be seen in the context of the Passover, when the Jews were asked to kill 'year-old male lambs without defects', and to place the blood of the freshly killed animal over the lintel and door-posts of their doorways.[19]

'That same night they are to eat the meat roasted over the fire, along with bitter herbs, and bread made without yeast.'[20]

Leaven, or yeast, is used throughout the Bible as a symbol of evil. The blood sacrifice and the marks on the doorway were a sign to the Lord to 'pass over' the household, sparing it from His destructive judgement — the death of all the first-born men and animals in Egypt.

In the New Testament accounts of the Last Supper, it is the death of Jesus that constitutes the blood sacrifice. Thus in the words of Luke:

> *After he took the bread, gave thanks and broke it, and gave it to them, saying, 'This is my body given for you; do this in remembrance of me.' In the same way, after supper he took the cup, saying; 'This cup is the new covenant in my blood, which is poured out for you.'*[21]

In contrast to the temporary atonement offered by Old Testament celebrations of the Passover, acceptance of the substitutional death of Jesus brings about permanent forgiveness of sin. I like the interpretation of Arnold Früchtenbaum, that the act of taking communion is like sprinkling the blood of Jesus over the lintel of one's heart as 'an insurance against sin'.

Unfortunately, in my experience this is not an absolute assurance. Ahh!

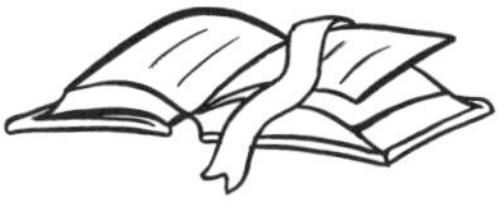

Tarta de Santiago

Saint James's Tart

Ingredients:

8 eggs
500 g sugar
400 g flour
250 g softened butter
1 tsp almond essence
1 glass water
250 g ground almonds
the finely chopped zest of two lemons
icing sugar for decoration

1. *In a mixing bowl, beat the eggs with the sugar to obtain a creamy mixture that holds its shape. Blend in the sifted flour, softened butter, almond essence and glass of water. Stir the mixture well.*
2. *Mix in the ground almonds and lemon peel, stirring until incorporated evenly through the mixture.*
3. *Pour into a circular, greased, 35 cm diameter tart mould or flan tin with fairly high sides. Bake in a moderate oven (180°C) for about 70 minutes or until ready.*
4. *Remove tart from the oven and leave to cool. Remove from the baking mould.*
5. *Cut out a piece of cardboard in the shape of the cross of Saint James. Place on the top and sprinkle the surface with icing sugar to decorate (sliced almonds may also be used). Remove the cardboard, leaving the sign of cross highlighted by outline of the icing sugar.*

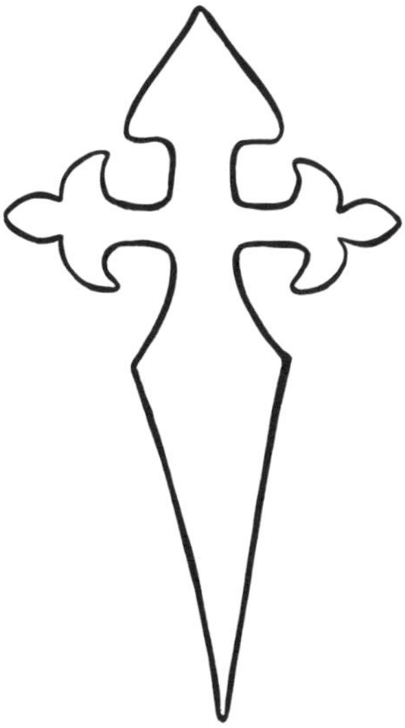

*R*eflexiones

Serendipity — the faculty of making happy and
unexpected discoveries by accident.

(The Concise Oxford Dictionary)

*P*rior to beginning the pilgrimage, we had been challenged as to why we should want to walk the best part of 1000 kilometres across a country at the veritable antipode to New Zealand. Now, with the walk behind us and basking in the sun in a cobblestoned square in Santiago after mass, it wasn't easy to put it all into perspective. Adventure, curiosity, spirituality, mid-life crises, or just plain fun? All these had been touted at home to explain our self-indulgence. The result had been much more, with the spiritual, historic, artistic, sociological and gastronomic dimensions of the pilgrim route each contributing towards a smorgasbord of experience. The camaraderie of the route, the generosity of the Spanish, and the routine of daily exercise had made it an unforgettable adventure.

In a world where the bad is so often emphasised, it had been nice to be reminded frequently of the intrinsic goodness of ordinary people. It had also been wonderful to shed the shackles and preoccupations of routine, and the dreary middle-class tendency of reducing life to a cash flow exercise. Security breeds its own malaise, and we had discovered other forms of exercise.

We felt great — well, mostly. Earlier we had tried to run across a busy street and had both nearly fallen flat on our faces. After walking steadily for near on five weeks our legs were incapable of moving any faster. Or perhaps it was just the absence of boots that left us unbalanced. All in all, it seemed much safer to rest seated outside a bar, nibbling on generous slices of *Tarte de Santiago* and soaking up the beer, the sound of guitars and the singing of students.

We felt alive: there is nothing bland about Spain — it excites all the senses. At the root of this excitement lies Spain's unique blend of regional differences in language, music, food and personality, the legacy of a collage of Iberian, Roman, Moorish, Jewish, and European influences. *El Camino* had offered us a taste panel of some of these differences.

Were we any better for having done this? That was hardly the point, and we are certainly not the best suited to adjudicate. At the time of writing our wives are still withholding judgement. They point to a significant but regrettably temporary weight loss — 10 kilograms in Pete's case and 3 for myself — as the only clearly demonstrative benefits. Pete claims that I cheated by taking only one stride to his two. Obviously overlooking these important second-order effects, I had calculated about 7.5 kilograms for us both.

On the spiritual side, the jury is still out. There were no specific visionary or inspirational experiences. But then according to Chaucer's Pardoner:

> – *All the victories,*
> *All the great deeds in the Old Testament*
> *Through the grace of God, Who is omnipotent,*
> *Were won by means of abstinence and prayer;*
> *Look in the Bible, and you'll find it there.*

Perhaps we had got the formula wrong. Despite this there had been a comforting sense of walking in the echoes of the footsteps of earlier pilgrims. A few theological questions were resolved, many more remain unanswered, and some may well be unanswerable. These categories mimic those of scientific enigmas — most are unattainable, a small proportion dangle tantalisingly just out of reach, whilst the remainder are of no real consequence.

Again, were we any better for having struggled with a few of life's mysteries? Who really cared? Pete and I had not seen this adventure in serendipity as an apprenticeship for selling indulgences. More importantly, we felt privileged to have supped from the cup of the fascination of Spain and, as for the future, well, perhaps we could take some encouragement from the Spanish proverb:

'You take the road, and the road makes you.'

Por Fin

Tell away, Roger, but mind it is good one;
For many's the stale pasty, drained of gravy,
And warmed-up Jack-of-Dover pie you've sold,
That's been twice hotted up and twice left cold.
Many's the pilgrim who has been the worse
For the parsley stuffing in your fatted goose,
And has called down upon you heaven's curse
Because your cookshop's always full of flies.

(The Canterbury Tales, *Geoffrey Chaucer*)

*&*ndnotes

1. Acts 12: 2
2. Pitte, J.P. (1991) *Gastronomie Française*. Fayard
3. Genesis 3.
4. Tate, R.B. (1990) *Pilgrimages to St. James of Compostella from the British Isles during the Middle Ages*. Liverpool University Press.
5. Starkie, W.F. (1957) *The Road to Santiago*. John Murray.
6. Romans 12: 19.
7. Hebrews 11: 6.
8. Lewis, C.S. (1952) *Mere Christianity*. Collins Fount Paperbacks.
9. Toussaint-Samat, M. (1993) *A History of Food*, translated by Anthea Bell, Blackwell Reference.
10. Barret, P. and Gurgand, J.N. (1978) *Priez Pour Nous à Compostelle*. Hachette.
11. ibid.
12. ibid.
13. Mabille de Poncheville, A. (1930) *Le Chemin de Saint Jacques*, Reprint de l'édition de 1930, Editions Kim à Rosendael-Lez-Dunkerque, (1989).
14. Popelin, C. (1970) *La Tauromachie*. Editions du Seuil.
15. Joubert, J.(1988) *Fabliaux et Contes du Moyen Age. Nouvelle Approache*. Le Livre de Poche.
16. Vermes, G. (1973) *Jesus the Jew. A historian's reading of the Gospels*. Collins.
17. Job 11: 7.
18. Mabille de Poncheville, A. (1930) *Le Chemin de Saint Jacques*, Reprint de l'édition de 1930, Editions Kim à Rosendael-Lez-Dunkerque, (1989).
19. Exodus 12.
20. ibid.
21. Luke 22: 17-19.